ALL ABOUT PROSPERITY

ALL ABOUT PROSPERITY

AND HOW

YOU CAN PROSPER

By Jack and Cornelia Addington

DEVORSS & COMPANY

P.O. Box 550

Marina del Rey, California 90294-0550

Library of Congress Catalog Number: 83-73342
ISBN: 0-87516-533-8

Cover design by Jeannie Branscomb

Printed in the United States of America

Hidden away in the inner nature of the real man is the law of his life and some day he will discover it and consciously make use of it. He will heal himself, make himself happy and prosperous, and will live in an entirely different world for he will have discovered that life is from within and not from without.

SPIRITUAL LAWS
by Ralph Waldo Emerson

One of the saddest experiences which can come to a human being is to awaken, gray-haired and wrinkled, near the close of an unproductive career, to the fact that all through the years he has been using only a small part of himself.

V. W. Burrows
from PETER'S QUOTATIONS

Beloved, I pray that you may prosper and be in health, just as your soul prospers.

III John, 1:2

Dedicated to those great men and women who,
down through the ages, have understood the laws
of prosperity and prospered to the glory of God
and all mankind.

CONTENTS

INTRODUCTION

Are you aware that there are definite laws of prosperity that you can use? Do you realize that your basic, everyday thinking can make you prosperous or keep you from prospering?

This book was written for those who would like to be prosperous as well as for those who would like to feel secure in their prosperity. It can be a mind-changer for you. To this end we would like to ask you a number of thought-provoking questions. Please read them slowly and think about each one with an open mind. For your own good, answer them honestly. Then, when you have finished reading the book, turn back to the Introduction and consider the questions again. Here are the questions:

What do you really believe about yourself?

Do you believe that you can be prosperous?

Or, do you believe you are destined to be poor?

Do you believe that it is right for you to prosper?

Do you believe that you are worthy of prosperity?

Do you believe that life wants you to prosper?

Do you believe that your basic thought about
yourself is important?

Do you believe that you have infinite resources
to draw upon as you move forward toward
a more fulfilling, creative and prosperous
life?

Our attitudes play such an important part in the
direction that our lives are taking. It is like pro-
gramming your home computer. Our attitudes program our thinking and our thinking directs the
course of our lives. An attitude is the stand we take
on any given matter. Let's take a look at some of
our attitudes and ask ourselves if we really want to
keep them.

What is your attitude toward prosperity?

Is your attitude one of acceptance or rejection?

Are you success oriented or failure oriented?

Can you identify yourself with prosperity as
a way of life?

Is your attitude one of revulsion toward
money?

Do you think of money as evil? filthy lucre?

Can you receive things from people, but not
money?

Do you have a habit pattern of continually
talking about hardship, bad times, your own
debts and losses? Are you willing to make
an about-face in this practice, talking "up"
instead of "poor-mouth"?

And lastly, there's the matter of acceptance.

Can you receive prosperity when it comes?

If we were to hand you prosperity in a package today, could you receive it, accept it for yourself?

Can you picture yourself as prosperous, successful in every area of living? Having every good thing in life?

Can you visualize yourself receiving large amounts of money, enjoying it, giving portions of it away freely?

Can you honestly claim for yourself: "I am prosperous; life prospers through me; I prosper in all that I do."

This book is designed to help the reader build a consciousness of prosperity. We believe that this is the master key to prosperous living. Money alone does not represent prosperity. Those who are rich but live in constant fear of losing their money are not truly prosperous. Mere possessions, not enjoyed, do not make one prosperous. Once one has the master key to enduring prosperity he or she can then enjoy prosperity with a feeling of inner security.

Remember, when you finish reading this book, we want you to go back and ask yourself the various questions in the Introduction again. See if your attitudes have changed.

Here's to an ever-expanding prosperity consciousness and an abundance of every good thing which it will surely bring you.

Jack and Cornelia Addington

Chapter I

PROSPERITY IS A
STATE OF MIND

Prosperity is a state of mind that carries over into every area of living—health, wealth, happiness and companionship. The word *wealth* comes from the root word *weal*, meaning *a state of well-being*.

Start now to develop a true prosperity consciousness and you will not only reap a rich harvest in your outer experience but with it will come a still greater blessing—*a sense of security which no one can ever take from you*. Your security is an inner condition that does not depend upon outer circumstances.

Through your belief, create a new image of yourself! Build an image of things working out well; think of yourself as a prosperous person. That which you believe about yourself will be fulfilled in your experience.

I know. You've heard that before. "That's cold comfort," you're thinking, "It's not going to pay the rent and the back taxes I owe, or get me the job that I need so badly."

1

Suppose I put it this way: Prosperity is a state of mind that makes itself known to you in every area of your life as abundant living.

To prosper, according to the dictionary, means *to be fortunate or successful; to thrive*. The person who has a feeling of prosperity has a feeling that life is working with him and not against him. The prosperity state of mind can produce not only an abundance of wealth but health and right action as well. When one arrives at an awareness of prosperity it flows over into every part of that person's experience so that he or she is prosperous over-all. One becomes prosperous in business, in family relationships, in romantic relationships and, generally, good health is a part of the package. Money is not the only evidence of prosperity thinking but it surely is one of the many by-products of a prosperity state of mind.

Henry Ford became a very wealthy man but that was not his objective. He once remarked that he set out to make the best car possible at the lowest price and the money came.

Recessions and Depressions Are Man-Made Not God-Ordained

If prosperity is a state of mind, then the opposite kind of thinking, such as poverty thinking, thoughts of failure, hard times, depressions and recessions are also states of mind, dangerous states of mind. We must beware of giving mental house room to such thoughts for they, too, will out-picture in the experience of life. *As within, so without, as above, so below*, is as meaningful today as it was back in the third century.

Ralph Waldo Emerson put it this way: *A man is what he thinks about twenty-four hours a day*. The Reverend Mr. Emerson had never heard of ERA but I am sure he meant his statement to include women, too.

Therefore, the master key to prosperity is to build a consciousness of prosperity and that is what this book is all about. Before you finish reading it you should not only be able to think prosperously but live prosperously. Remember, you cannot afford to go back to your old negative thinking patterns. We cannot, any of us, afford to entertain thoughts of lack, thoughts of recessions, thoughts of poverty of any kind. We must completely disregard the doom and gloom sayers who prophesy continuing hard times.

Anthony Santangelo came to the United States from Italy because he had heard that it was the land of opportunity. He firmly believed that every-one in America gets rich. And so it was for him. It seemed that Tony and his wife Maria just couldn't fail. Everything they did prospered.

They started out by setting up a hamburger stand in front of the little farm they bought on the edge of town. There was no question about it. Their hamburgers were special. Soon they were adding fresh homemade bread and rolls and a counter of fancy pastries. Maria had to get up at four in the morning to keep up with the demand but she didn't mind. It was fun and she loved talking to the people who stopped at their place. Their following grew and grew by word of mouth. People came from far distances just to eat at Tony's Place.

Success breeds success and soon they had a very attractive restaurant with red checkered table cloths and fresh flowers on every table. Tony and Maria worked hard but they loved it. They planned to add gift items and a little antique shop on the side. Everything continued to prosper. They were able to send their son to college and hire an extra cook in the kitchen. They even added a gardener and the place became more and more beautiful. Plans were in the making for a new house to replace the little cottage where they lived. They couldn't wait to show Tony Jr. when he came home from college for Christmas vacation.

And then everything changed. Tony Jr. was shocked. "Don't you know that there's a depression?" he asked them. "Times are bad everywhere. Don't you ever read the newspapers?"

His parents had to admit they hadn't had time to read a paper in months. They were so busy building up the business that they hadn't had time. Tony and Maria talked it over. After all, their son had been to college. He was studying business management. He ought to know. They had better listen to him. Maybe they *should* prepare for a depression. And so reluctantly they started to cut back. They cancelled the plans for the new house which was a blow to the architect and the local builder who decided they'd have to cut back also. Yes, times were bad. If Tony who was always so optimistic was worried maybe they should let some of their help go, too. Tony gave up his dream of a small gift and antique shop and cancelled his order from a specialty house. He wouldn't need the souvenirs and gift items he had planned to add to his restaurant. This was a great disappointment to the young salesman who had been working with him and he told everyone he saw from then on that the depression was here. Why, even Mr. Santangelo was feeling it.

It wasn't fun to go to Tony's Place anymore. Tony and Maria looked so sad that their former customers began to avoid them. The business began to fall off more and more as the weeks went on. Soon they let the cook go and gave up selling the fresh bakery goods. The cook was a widow who had counted on her job to support her five children. What was she to do now? She passed the word along to everyone. "Yes, business is bad, very bad. The restaurant is failing."

The gardener was the next to go. They no longer needed fresh fruit and vegetables since they had cut back on the menu. The gardener had counted on the work to supplement his small retirement and he was quick to tell his friends and relatives that business was poor and times were bad.

The depression was here. At least in their community. News travels fast. Everyone who stopped at Tony's Place heard the gloomy news and passed it on. Like a snowball, it gathered momentum and more and more people were affected.

In the end, the depression turned out to be a false rumor which had been started as political progaganda but by the time Tony found this out, he didn't have the heart to start over and many people had been hurt. The moral of this story is: *Don't listen to bad news. Life is an individual experience. Each one must live out of his own consciousness.* As long as Tony believed he would succeed, nothing could stop him.

People make depressions. People make prosperity or failure by their attitudes. It makes no difference what the state of the economy is reputed to be there are always those who are able to succeed. Some will always get good jobs and prosper in whatever they do. They are the people who maintain a prosperity state of mind. It isn't always easy when negative thinking is thrown at us from every side but it pays rich dividends.

Thought-Watching Your Way to Prosperity

We have to be diligent thought-watchers, allowing into our minds only those thoughts that carry the right credentials. Like the door-keeper at some big event who allows only those people to enter who have the right ticket, we must allow only those thoughts to enter our minds that belong to the prosperity state of mind we are working to achieve.

For example: Instead of saying "It can't work, times are bad, nobody will buy our product," we have to rule out the failure thoughts and ask ourselves, "How *can* we make this project work?"

The important thing is to get our minds away from our own little sneaky fears of lack and start realizing abundance for ourselves and others. What happens? Then we will start to manifest abundance in our own lives. *That to which we give our attention always grows and multiplies*. This is a law of life.

The Secret of Prosperous Living

So, now we are going to give our attention to prosperous living. Prosperous living means:

1. That we are working with life and life is working with us.
2. That we are drawing upon life's riches and life is responding to us.
3. That we are thinking positively and, therefore, having positive results.
4. That we are trusting in the Perfect Power within and, therefore, being guided into right action.
5. That we can trust and know that the Perfect Power within is taking care of us and we no longer need to worry.

Once we understand the meaning of prosperous living, a change comes over us. Now, we are able to meet the vicissitudes of life with confidence and assurance. We are no longer in bondage to our fears. We are able to walk in the light, rather than in darkness. We are able to be creative, thereby consciously creating circumstances in accord with right thinking and right living. Once we understand them, we are able to apply the laws of life in our daily living. It is as if we had emerged from a maze and established ourselves on a high viewpoint from which we could see the truth about ourselves and life itself. Now we know: *It is done unto you as you believe*.

Already everything seems different. The world looks a little brighter. Having lifted our sights and rerouted our thinking into prosperity channels, we are able to be aware of the infinite potential within. We let our minds become creative and imaginative, expanding our mental horizons. Prosperous thinking is expansive thinking. As we said before, it is not limited strictly to money and business, but reflects into every area of living. When we start out thinking that we have an infinite Source to draw from, we prosper in our human relationships, our marriages prosper and this spills over into our physical well-being, so that we find that good health is a part of this new way of life. It is all a package. We cannot have a healing in one area without it reflecting into all areas.

So, as you begin this program of building an enduring prosperity consciousness, prepare to receive health, happiness, and well-being in many areas of living. It works that way. We have been given dominion, spiritual dominion. Whatever we believe about ourselves is how life is going to respond to us.

Now, forget the past and all of your reactions to the past. Start right this moment believing that the Perfect Power right within you is able to do all things for you in perfect ways. Remember, the secret is: *turn away from your old problems and start thinking about the abundance of life, about the ability of the Perfect Power within you to accomplish all things in right and perfect ways.* Start entertaining these ideas. Let them take root in your deep consciousness.

This is a mind-training program in which we are going to replace old, negative patterns with positive, affirmative patterns. To help you do this we are going to give you Self-Direction affirmations at the end of each chapter. Use them over and over until they become part of you. Eventually, they will root out of you the thoughts you would like to be rid of and you will find yourself habitually thinking thoughts that belong to a prosperity state of mind.

Self-Direction for a Prosperity State of Mind

Today I give my attention to divine Abundance and
   my good flows in from every side.
The Infinite has enough and to spare for us all;
   I do not have to envy those who have more than
   I do.
Turning within for ideas, I receive ideas that bless
   and prosper me.
I have a consciousness of success and abundance; I
   can envision myself no other way and so I attract
   success.

I do not judge abundance by appearances for I know that as I expand my inner awareness the outer will manifest as abundance.

I am in tune with prosperity. I accept prosperity in every area of my life.

And so it is.

Chapter II

SOME PRACTICAL STEPS THAT WILL HELP YOU BUILD A PROSPERITY CONSCIOUSNESS

Start right where you are with what you have. "But," you say, "I don't have anything."

That's what the widow said to Elisha when he asked her what she had in the house, "I have nothing."

"Come now, you must have something," he urged. Finally, she admitted that she did have a little pot of oil. So the great prophet told her to start with what she had. She was instructed to send her sons out to borrow from the neighbors all of the vessels they could find and he cautioned her "not a few." And when they borrowed the vessels they were to pour from that little pot of oil until they were all full. And what do you know! The oil did not stop flowing until every vessel was full. Then, Elisha told her to sell the oil and pay her debts and live with her boys on the rest of the money.

There's such a wonderful lesson here. The vessels that they borrowed represent their measure of faith.

11

Had they borrowed twice as many they would have had twice as much oil to sell. And so it is with us. We set our own limitations.

You can take a cup or a bucket to the sea and fill it with water. The sea does not question the size of your vessel. Nor does the sea of universal consciousness question the size of your faith. According to your measure of consciousness, it is measured to you.

What do you have? Right where you are is a mine of resources more valuable than gold. You have creative imagination. You have intuition to guide you and creativity to build beautiful buildings and paint gorgeous pictures. Right within you is a reservoir of love and understanding that can overcome any problem and inspiration that will move men's hearts as well as mountains. Start with what you have and move confidently forward.

Some Practical Steps To Help You Get Started

The first step is to marshal all of your assets: spiritual, mental and physical. Do you really know what you have? It might be well to make an inventory, being careful not to overlook any hidden assets. You might even have some valuable insurance policies that you thought had lapsed.

I once had a friend who was a very successful life insurance agent. He sold more insurance than anybody I've ever known before or since. One of the things that he did was to have his clients search out their hiding places for important papers and look for lapsed life insurance policies. Even though policies were lapsed they still had a cash value. It was surprising how many people cashed in thousands of dollars from policies that had been lapsed, five, ten, and twenty years. He helped them dig up old stocks and bonds that they had thought were worthless. He had his clients make an inventory of their jewelry, antiques, silver and anything else that might have value. Before he got through he had convinced them that they were worth more than they thought they were.

More than likely you are worth more than you think. You may find that your house is filled with valuable antiques. You may have valuable paintings stashed away in the attic. Those old Chinese bowls that Grandma left you may be worth five hundred dollars each. That old coin collection Uncle Ben gave you when you were a child may be worth a great deal today and the old gold jewelry you never really liked may now be very saleable and worth far more to you invested in some other way. A set of sterling silver flatware lying unused in a drawer may be worth thousands of dollars today. Old newspapers and first editions of books have been found to be worth a fortune. You may be richer than you ever dreamed and as you marshal your assets your prosperity consciousness will grow.

An aunt of mine down in Houston, Texas, reached that point in life where she felt it was necessary to go into a retirement home. She wondered if she could afford it. Her principal asset was her little house in which she had lived for fifty years. Alas, it was surrounded by tall office buildings and she questioned whether anyone would want it. Imagine her surprise when the real estate agent said he thought it would sell right away. She wound up getting nearly a million dollars for it.

A friend of mine was called to be the minister of a church in Oklahoma. When he first walked through the church edifice he was appalled that such an attractive building had been allowed through neglect to deteriorate so badly. He took the matter up with the Board and was told that the church just didn't have the money to redecorate, buy new draperies and do all of the things the new pastor thought were needed. It was a sad beginning to his new assignment. He prayed about it. An inspiration came to him. He decided to talk to the church treasurer. He was told about various funds that were earmarked for, believe it or not, projects that had long since been abandoned. To his amazement he found about $6,000 loafing, enough and to spare to do all that was needed.

Check Out Your Options

Never take it for granted that you have only one way to go. You may have more viable options than you think. As you open your mind to consider your various opportunities, new ideas will come to you. The best way to do this is to take a pencil and a sheet of paper and start writing down options. Do not consider these *your* options but *the* options available to meet the situation. If you consider them *your* options you will be apt to judge them and rule them out before you write them down.

A young mother left alone with several young children was starting out on a new job and needed transportation badly. Unfortunately, it had taken every cent she had to pay the first and last month's rent and the cleaning charge on the apartment she had just rented. What was she to do? She wrote out her options. 1. The perfect, right transportation for me exists. 2. There is a right car for me. 3. There is a car that I can afford to buy. She didn't dare examine that third option because at the moment she didn't have a dime in her pocket. The next week a friend of hers called and said, "I hear you're needing an automobile." This, at first, seemed like an answer to prayer. However, the car was worth $500 and the owner wanted at least $100 down. It might as well have been $1,000! She just didn't have it. This was an opportunity she would have to pass up. So, she went back to her third option—"a car I can afford to buy." She refused to allow herself to become discouraged.

Almost immediately the answer came. One of her co-workers told her about a car that she could buy for $125 and it was in excellent condition. It had new tires and a new motor and had been kept in tip top shape. The owner was willing to sell it to her without a down payment. This seemed like a miracle. It actually happened. Had our friend not written down her options without judging them she might never have recognized this opportunity.

Accept the Best and You Will Have the Best

A young man was eating from a plate of grapes when the rabbi came to call. He asked the rabbi, "Shouldn't I always save the best grapes for the last?"

The rabbi surprised him by saying, "Always eat the best first, and you'll always be eating the best."

How many times we save our best clothes until they are out of style and then wind up hardly getting to wear them at all!

When my grandmother died at 98 her daughters found that all the lovely things they had sent mother over the years, the hand-embroidered handkerchiefs, the lace-trimmed nightgowns and slips had never been worn. Their mother felt they were too good for every day wear and kept saving them year after year for a worthy occasion. Always use the best first and you will always have the best — store them away and it is just as if you never had them.

Try dressing up now and then. Wear your best clothes. You'll find that when you look prosperous you will not only feel prosperous but you will think prosperous thoughts that will go to work for you and bring prosperity into your experience.

Clean Out Your Attic And Sort Out Your Closets

We all need to get the clutter out of our lives. Why hang on to a lot of old clothes and other things that you will never use again. Let them be someone else's demonstration. Stop hanging onto things for a rainy day. Feel good about sharing with others. The room that you make in your closet will soon be filled with new clothes that will lift your spirits and be part of your new prosperity. Being generous will make you feel prosperous. Feeling prosperous will bring you the prosperity experience.

When is a Saving a Saving?

It's fine to save money but beware of impoverishing yourself in the process. Ask yourself, "Does my scrounging really pay off?"

I have in mind a young couple who thought they'd beat the rap by doing their own moving. Having bought a home on the other side of the mountains, they couldn't bear to pay the moving charge involved in moving a houseful of furniture. So, they rented a truck and did it themselves. Six trips they made across the mountains before they were through. When the move was finally accomplished, they totaled up the cost and found to their amazement that it had cost much more to do it the way they did. Not to mention the back-breaking effort and all the time involved.

This works out in so many areas. I know a man
who has plenty of money. He can well afford to
travel by plane, yet he chooses to drive his car across
the continent in order to save money. He and his
wife drive night and day, alternating sleep cycles.
If they do stop they stay in the cheapest motels they
can find, dirty, rundown places inhabited by cock-
roaches and other vermin. He loses a lot of time
traveling this way, time that might be worth more
than the dollar saving. Apparently this is all he can
accept for himself. He just does not have a prosperity consciousness. How much better it would be
to stretch a little. If he were to travel by plane he
might not only save time but money in the last
analysis. Moreover, he could use the time on the
plane to build a prosperity consciousness!

We all know people who have scrimped all
through life so that they could afford to travel when
they retired. And then, at retirement age, the stress
of their grim way of life caught up with them and
because of health problems they were unable to
travel at all.

Do you expect the best or do you always settle for
third rate? Ralph Buford lived in New Orleans
around the turn of the century. In those days the
best way to get from Boston to New Orleans was by
ship. So Ralph, having concluded a not too successful business trip to Boston, spent the last of his
money on a steamship ticket to New Orleans. After
he had booked his passage he had just enough
money left to get some cheese and crackers. "Well,

at least I won't starve on the way home," he thought. And so he carefully avoided the dining room throughout the entire trip.

On the last day as the passengers stood on the deck waiting to disembark, one of them spoke to Ralph. "We haven't seen you in the dining room this trip," he remarked.

Ralph flushed with embarrassment.

"The meals were great," his companion went on, "but, where were you?"

"No," Ralph confessed, more embarrassed than ever, "I just didn't have the means. I brought along some food and ate in my stateroom."

His fellow traveler looked up puzzled, "But, the meals were all included in the fare!" he said.

Ralph had a consciousness of lack. He was unable to accept his good. I daresay he had gone through life that way which probably accounted for his lack of success in business. How many of us go through life passing up the good things to which we are entitled because we do not claim our good? Our motto should be: *Use the best and you will always have the best because you will be building a prosperity consciousness as you go.*

Expect the Best and You Will Get the Best

The master key to prosperity is *build a consciousness of prosperity.* I have been teaching this for many years and out of the hundreds of testimonial letters I have received from people joyfully telling me how it worked for them, I only recall one that strongly stated, "It doesn't work for me!" And then he told me why: "I never expect anything," he wrote, "and I'm never disappointed." Does that tell you something? It does me.

We have to expect the best in order to receive the best. Start by knowing that consciousness is the only reality. If you have a consciousness of success, that which you accept for yourself will become your experience. If you desire to prosper, know that prosperity is a matter of having a prosperity consciousness. Once you have established a prosperity consciousness, nothing can take it away from you. You will never lack any good thing.

Even though you lose everything through some catastrophe such as fire, flood, or robbery, in some magical way it will be restored to you. You may have to start over, but sooner or later, you will look around you at your possessions and note that you have everything just as attractive and right for you as you had before. That which you claim for yourself by right of consciousness will always evolve out of the "mind stuff" into your experience. Sir Arthur Eddington called it "mind stuff." And that is what it is, the substance out of which the manifest world is made. Expect the best, and you will get the best. Expect to prosper and you will.

Self-Direction

I expect the best and receive the best.

Only good goes from me and only good returns to
me.

My Father is a millionaire. He wants me to have
the best.

He wants me to go first class.

I accept the best and use the best without guilt or
regret.

I release the past knowing that Principle is not
bound by precedent.

I am supplied out of the wealth of Infinite
Abundance.

And so it is.

Chapter III

WHO ARE THE RICH?
WHO ARE THE POOR?

Before we go any further we should ask ourselves, "Is the possession of money or things the criterion of prosperity?"

My answer to that question is, "absolutely not." My files are loaded with news items concerning people who literally starved to death with a fortune concealed about them. Here are a few of these stories selected at random. You've probably read similar ones in your local newspaper.

There is an instance of a North Miami woman who lived in a rubble-strewn cottage and starved to death. Her cottage, cluttered with debris and refuse, disclosed a handbag stuffed with twenty $1,000 bills, and bonds and securities with a total current market value of $80,000. That woman starved to death because she wasn't using that which she had.

In New York, a woman who lived in a fire-damaged apartment and dined on hot dogs, died of malnutrition with $274,980 in cash under her bed and another quarter of a million dollars in banks. The inclination is to think of her as just being crazy and dismiss the incident. However, it is only another case of insecurity. What is the difference between a person dying of starvation with ten dollars on him as against one with a million dollars? One is more dramatic than the other, that is all.

In California several years ago, a man was arrested for jaywalking. He was in ragged clothing and was unkempt. The arresting officer became suspicious when he noticed that he had something pinned inside his clothing. The man was taken to the police station and searched. They found two rolls of $1,000 bills amounting to $212,000 pinned in his ragged clothing. He did not trust banks. It was legitimately his money, but he did not possess it in consciousness. Do you see the difference?

Who Had the Consciousness of Abundance?

I came upon this story in the Denver Post a few years ago when I was visiting in Denver. The headline was: POOR LITTLE OLD LADY'S ESTATE, $285,000 PLUS. They thought Mrs. Mary Margaret Frazer was a poor little old lady, but her will was full of surprises. She died February 18, in a hospital ward because they thought she couldn't afford a private room. She was in her 70's. Dr. Louis Scarone, believing her indigent, had treated her for three years without ever sending a bill. She was the widow of a British Royal Air Force

Colonel and lived alone in a mid-town hotel. She used to gather left-over food at dinner parties and take it to her room. But lawyer Harold Baker, as executor, was distributing her estate, and it was estimated by the court at $285,000 cash, plus a jewel collection of unestimated value. A news report on her will said Dr. Scarone was to get $50,000. The hospital $10,000. She left $50,000 to a super-market produce manager who was nice to her. She left $25,000 to one of the hotel maids, $50,000 to another. The news report said that there were plenty of funds to take care of all the bequests she made.

Now, the question in my mind is *who had the consciousness of abundance in this case?* It's a fascinating story, isn't it? Here this little lady was treated as an indigent, accepted this status, when all the time she had *over a quarter of a million dollars in cash!* Was she the one who demonstrated this wealth? Was it wealth to her? Did she have a consciousness of abundance? True, she had all that she needed. If people wanted to think of her as poverty stricken it apparently made no difference to her. She knew she had the cash in the bank. Evidently, she had no desire to use money. To her, it wasn't money in the sense that it could be used to obtain that which she needed.

But, how about those who inherited under her will? What about the doctor who treated her for nothing? Just think, for three whole years he gave his services for nothing. He never sent her a bill.

$50,000 was what he got for his services. $10,000 went to the hospital and $50,000 to the man at the supermarket who was kind to her. He probably gave her leftover produce! The interesting thing, to me, is that these people gave to her with no thought of return. They gave with no strings attached and it came back to them. They received richly.

Fear of Poverty Is Poverty Itself

We can quickly see that fear of poverty is really worse than being what the world calls poor.

Here is another story that gives us food for thought. It appeared in the San Diego Union some years ago.

"An elderly Point Loma widow, who said she had been carrying around a fortune in a package because she distrusted banks, told today how she lost $85,000 last night. Mrs. Amine Hicks, about 70, told police she laid a bulky package containing the cash on the counter of a drugstore. She said she was buying some fluid to clean the suit she wore and left the store without picking up the paper-wrapped package of $50 and $100 bills. The money was in packets of $1,000 each.

"Mrs. Hicks said today she discovered the loss when she got home a few minutes later. The druggist, who had closed the store, reopened late last night but the package of money was missing."

The article is very long. I can't possibly quote it all, although it is extremely interesting. To my knowledge, the woman never recovered her money. There were no clues. The article went on to say that she had left it in other places at other times, but had always recovered it before. Whenever she went out she carried the $85,000 in a bulky, string-tied package because she distrusted banks.

"Money is a curse," she said. "Everyone's trying to get it away from you."

So I ask you: Here was a woman who had $85,000 in cash that she carried with her wherever she went, but, was she rich or was she poor?

The Bible says: *To him that hath shall be given and to him who hath not shall be taken away even that which he hath.*

What does this mean? To me it means that if you don't have a consciousness of prosperity you will lose whatever you have.

Poverty Is a State of Mind

Take Bertha Adams; she died alone at 71 from malnutrition after wasting away to 50 pounds. Bertha had been in the habit of begging for food at the back doors of her neighbors. Her house looked like a pigpen and she got what clothes she had as handouts from the Salvation Army. Imagine people's surprise when she left behind a fortune of nearly $1,000,000, including approximately $800,000 in cash and $40,000 in stocks. Yes, she was starving to death and yet she wouldn't spend any money to get something to eat. I ask you, was she rich or was she poor?

This, of course, is an extreme example, but in a smaller way, I know a great many people who are doing without the comforts of life, living frugally, when all the time they could not possibly spend the money they have in a lifetime. They continue to save and scrimp in order to accumulate wealth which they will not use. It ceases to be money except on paper. Yes, as we have said so many times, *consciousness is the only reality, and both prosperity and poverty are states of mind.*

The Law of Life is impersonal. It does not care which you choose — success or failure. You can have it either way. Prosperity is much more than the acquisition of mere material things. Prosperity is the ability to achieve; to be what you want to be; to do what you would like to do; the ability to express your God-given talents; the ability to draw upon the infinite resources of God right where you are and make them a part of your own experience. Prosperity is a matter of accomplishing. It is the attainment of the objective desired. It is well-being as opposed to adversity.

Why the Rich Are Often Poor

Prosperity is not just a matter of accumulating lots of money. We all know people who have done this and remained poor. The possession of money is a relative thing. There are those who are multi-millionaires, yet they are paupers at heart. Many people become so engrossed in accumulating money that they lose sight of the true values in life. They worry so much about hanging on to their money that they lose the kingdom of God within.

On the other hand, I know people who have so little of what the world considers wealth that they would be classed as "poor people" by some, yet they have everything they need and more, so that they are completely happy. I consider them prosperous because they are achieving and accomplishing that which they truly desire, and doing so with peace of mind. What more could anyone ask?

Now Let Us Ask Ourselves: Who Are the Rich? Who Are the Poor?

Is a person prosperous who has a fortune in the bank which he never touches although he denies himself a great deal to keep the money intact? Is a person prosperous who has a large income but lives so far beyond his means that he is always in debt? And how about the person who has a generous income, yet envies everyone who makes more than he does? Is that person prosperous? Or, the person who is fearful of losing his investment and worries constantly over the fluctuating market? What about retired people who seem to have all that they need and live comfortably on their Social Security or other retirement income? Are they not richer than many who have more stashed away which they cannot bring themselves to use?

Self-Direction

I will have faith, not fear. Through faith I build
a kingdom of inner security.

I am blessed with wisdom in the use of the resources
that come to me. I use what I have freely
knowing that my supply is continuous.

I renounce poverty and accept prosperity as my way
of life.

Infinite Intelligence within guides me into channels
of right activity.

Refusing to identify with lack, I continue to see
abundance everywhere.

I give freely and receive joyfully from a consciousness of abundance.

And so it is.

Chapter IV

PITFALLS TO PROSPERITY AND HOW TO OVERCOME THEM

It may be that you have become trapped in one of the pitfalls to prosperity. If so, remember there is a way out. Forget your pride for a few moments, and, if the shoe fits, put it on. Start working your way out of any particular pitfall which applies to you. These pitfalls to prosperity are very subtle and are often emotional. You must be completely honest with yourself for if you allow yourself to become trapped in one of these pitfalls, all is lost — you will never demonstrate prosperity.

Pitfall Number One:

Trying to get something for nothing.

It is always a mistake to try to get something for nothing, or something at the expense of someone else. We all know Freddy the Freeloader. Freddy never has any money in his billfold and when his turn comes to pick up the tab he manages to become very engrossed in something else. One fellow I know always carries a tooth brush in his pocket, and when he sees that the tab is to be presented, he escapes to the men's room to brush his teeth! Freddy frequently borrows from his friends but never intends to pay them back. Eventually, he is no longer invited to make up a golf foursome and nobody wants him to share in a vacation weekend. He thinks he is getting ahead this way, but a little thought will give you the clue to his poverty — he thinks of himself as getting by without spending money. Every time he gets by with having someone else pick up his lunch tab, he may think he's winning, but all the time he's really losing. He's setting himself up mentally for a self-addressed future order of: *I can't make it on my own: I have to depend on someone else to pay my way in life.* If Freddy only knew that it would be just as easy to be generous, he could pay his own way and have plenty.

The Prosperity Solution

God is my supply, an infinite Source right within me. All that I need flows through me. I dare to give generously for I know that I can never outgive God.

Pitfall Number Two:

Feeling unworthy to receive one's good.

It is surprising how many people feel unworthy to receive their good. A young man wrote me the other day that he felt guilty to eat three meals a day when there were so many people starving in the world. At first, this sounds like a loving approach, a high consideration for the welfare of others. But is it? Self-condemnation in any form is never a healthy mental state. If one would help others, let him demonstrate the wherewithal to give to others who may be needy. There is no virtue in getting down and groveling in the ditch with the less fortunate.

A young man in New York who inherited a fortune and threw it away in the streets that he might himself become poor accomplished no lasting good. He simply established the fact that he did not have a consciousness of receiving his inheritance. Good stewardship requires that we accept the responsibility to use what is entrusted to us in a wise and intelligent way.

No man is an island, entire of itself; every man is a piece of the continent, a part of the maine, wrote John Donne. Never were truer words spoken, especially when it comes to the economy. Every time we make a purchase in the supermarket, we help provide for someone else. When people stop buying automobiles there is a chain reaction and the economy suffers all the way down the line. Every dollar we put into circulation helps someone pay the rent and buy food for his family. Every part helps a part. Your success contributes to the success of others. Those who try to be poor in order to help others only succeed in increasing the tax load for the hard-working who foot the bill for welfare and unemployment. The best thing you can possibly do to help others is, believe it or not, to be successful yourself. Personal austerity, far from being a virtue, only keeps money out of circulation and contributes to a mass consciousness of lack.

The Prosperity Solution

Recognizing myself as a child of God, I accept my spiritual heritage. I am complete, whole and entire and lacking in nothing. I accept God's abundance entrusted to me and use it wisely.

Pitfall Number Three:

The Paradox of the pocketbook protector.

The pocketbook protector's motto is: *Never spend a dime if you can help it*. He's willing to go without things that he really needs and can well afford in order not to spend money.

Have you ever solicited contributions for a church or charity? You approach a person who is known to be very well-to-do. Just as soon as you mention your mission, his hand automatically goes to the wallet pocket and gently rests over the opening so that the wallet cannot get out. The pocketbook protector generally keeps his change in a small snap purse. Moths are said to fly out of it when it is opened. It also is kept tightly buttoned into the pocket. This person is a getter but not a giver. He is said to have the first nickel he ever made, for one of his principles is never to give back into life. Why is this philosophy a pitfall? Because the pocketbook protector always feels poor and this keeps his increase from coming to him. Because he cannot bear to spend money, he misses the joy of having money. In the end it is just as if he had no money.

The Prosperity Solution

I give to life and life gives back to me. I am a channel for God's infinite good. That which I give away comes back to me multiplied.

Pitfall Number Four:

Making an enemy out of one's competitor.

One pitfall we are apt to pass by is often disguised as a great American virtue. It is commonly called competition. *All's fair in love and war*, they say, and many think this applies to business. There are those who feel justified in going to any length to get rid of a competitor. They lie about him to the customers, keep him from getting merchandise, in short, cause him to fail if possible. This is not the way to prosper. Sooner or later, to quote Edwin Markham: *All that we give into the lives of others comes back into our own.*

When one strives against another to gain the same objective it is bound to cause stress and a feeling of lack. Our good does not depend upon competition. Each one must live out of his own consciousness. It is fallacious to think we must take from someone else. In the game of life the winner is always the one who does the best that he can with what he has. This applies in the business world, too. All too often a businessman will pay so much attention to what another business is doing that he loses sight of his own creativity, his own potential. When one competes only with himself, endeavoring continually to be the best expression of that self, everything works out fine.

I once asked a friend of mine who was the Chairman of the Board of a large grocery chain how his company felt about their competition. He replied: "Oh, we know what they are doing, but we don't let what they are doing govern us. We give the best merchandise at the best price, with the best service, and we hire the best people. Every year we grow and prosper. We let our competition compete against us." Throughout the years this company has conducted its business on this basis and they have continued to prosper.

The Prosperity Solution

I bless the business across the street for I know there is no competition in my mind. His success is my success. His good is my good. The success he is able to manifest is also possible for me. I rejoice in his good and welcome it into my own experience.

Pitfall Number Five:

Getting yours while the getting's good.

This pitfall results from the belief that the reservoir of good is about to run out, that the supply of whatever you might need is limited; therefore, you must grab yours now in order to get your share.

Gertie the Grabber endeavors to get her good away from others because she thinks that the supply is not going to last. She's a hoarder. She eats more than she needs to be sure that she gets her share. She carries a shopping bag with her to pick up those extra rolls and crackers left on the table and her closets are loaded with things she can no longer wear but hangs onto because she might need them someday. Gertie is like the Dead Sea—she's stagnant because she has no outlet. She saves old postcards, old newspapers; everything piles up around her because she keeps fearing that rainy day when she just might need these things. Gertie needs a good housecleaning, mentally and physically, so that she can be a free channel for life's unlimited resources.

The Prosperity Solution

Life's free-flowing abundance is mine, to use and to share. I need no longer store it up for there is fresh manna for tomorrow.

Pitfall Number Six:

*The leaners who dare not trust
the Perfect Power within.*

Leaners lack self-confidence. They are afraid to strike out for themselves and cling to the family out of a sense of insecurity. You'd be surprised how many men and women live out their entire lives under the parental roof, afraid to venture forth from the nest. In this group we find men who marry surrogate mamas who will support them. Likewise, some women marry father images who continue to baby them and relieve them of all responsibility.

One might also place in this group a number of people, both men and women, who are receiving permanent disability payments. Many dare not get well or the payments will stop. Therefore, they pass up any possibility of prospering in their own right. It's a vicious circle and not a happy one.

There are others who look to the government for their security. Here we have the second and third generation welfare recipients who are afraid to venture forth on their own. The government becomes their surrogate parent. Today we are finding that when an able-bodied welfare recipient can be encouraged to learn a trade and step out into the stream of life he becomes transformed. A new light comes into his eye, a new confidence possesses him as he begins to trust in the Perfect Power within.

The Prosperity Solution

I trust in the Lord with all my heart. God in me is able to provide for me through me, and lead me into paths of right action. I step forth confidently. There is a right and perfect place for me to express in life. I am successful in all that I do.

Pitfall Number Seven:

Hating to pay the bills and the taxes.

Here's a pitfall that we have all been guilty of: hating to pay the bills; hating to pay those taxes; putting off writing the checks as long as possible because we hate to see our bank account diminished. This is a subtle snare one should be aware of and try to correct. It stems from a mistaken belief that our Source will become diminished; that there is no more where our present supply came from; and, sad as it seems, shows a lack of love for others. When we hate to pay for goods and services we are not wanting to share with others what is justly theirs. The spiritual growth here comes in being glad to see the butcher and the baker and the candlestick maker make a good living.

We have a little game that we play at our house. When we write our checks instead of writing 00/100's after the dollars, we write 00/xxx and we know as we write those three little xxx's that they mean "God is Abundance." My wife and I have done this for many years. It is to us a constant reminder to trust in the One Source that is never diminished and provides a blessing for every check that is written.

The Prosperity Solution

I gladly pay this bill with a special blessing for the receiver. I am happy to see others prosper, to be a part of another's prosperity answer. I gladly pay my taxes. Instead of thinking of government expenditures with which I disagree, I give my attention to all of the good public works with which I can agree. I bless each check as it goes on its way, knowing that that which I am able to give freely will come back to me in the same way.

Pitfall Number Eight:

Fear of losing what we have will keep us from being prosperous.

Every now and then we hear of people who are so fearful of losing their wealth that they neither trust banks nor their own hiding places.

Anything that involves fear will keep us from prospering. Even a little fear of banks and the economy will cause us to tighten up and actually be afraid to succeed. People who are afraid of banks and hide their wealth are apt to draw to themselves the very disaster they fear.

Did you ever hear the story of the woman who said that the last place a person would look for money was in the old wood stove that no one used anymore? She herself burned up her life savings when she forgot momentarily that she put it there and decided to have a little fire on a chilly night.

In the first place, the money becomes dead in that it is not working by drawing interest or dividends or giving employment to others. It is like the parable of the talents where the man who was given one talent and hid it, had it taken away by the Lord with the admonition that he who has, will be given more and he who has not will have it all taken away. Life will give to you according to how you give to life.

The Prosperity Solution

My supply does not belong to me personally. I only use it while I'm here. Nothing can be taken away from me that rightfully belongs to me by right of consciousness. My supply is from God. It flows freely from a never-ending Source. I need not fear for the morrow when I know that my good can never be cut off.

Pitfall Number Nine:

Thinking that there is some virtue in poverty and that, therefore, those who have money are to be despised and condemned.

There are those who think it a Christian virtue to be poor. This attitude arises from several statements made by Jesus. In the book of Matthew, we find him saying to his disciples: *Verily I say unto you that a rich man shall hardly enter into the kingdom of heaven.* He had just been asked by a young man, *Good Master, what good thing shall I do, that I may have eternal life?* When questioned by Jesus, the young man admitted that he had kept all of the commandments, but still felt he lacked something.

Jesus told him, *If thou wilt be perfect, go and sell what thou hast, and give to the poor, and thou shalt have treasure in heaven, and come and follow me. But the young man went away sorrowful for he had great possessions.*

Obviously, Jesus sensed that this young man was putting his material possessions ahead of his spiritual life; that he was making a god of his riches. As Dr. Ernest Holmes used to say so very often: *If anything comes between you and your divine fulfillment, it is a false god; get rid of it!*

The Bible does not say that money is the root of all evil. It says the *love of money* is the root of all evil. The Bible also says, *they shall prosper that love thee.*

People who have this attitude may secretly envy those who are prosperous and at the same time console themselves by feeling self-righteous. They often feel virtuous in resenting others who have more of this world's good than they. Resenting or coveting what another has impoverishes the self and builds a continual consciousness of lack.

Every good gift cometh from above. Prosperity represents the grace of God in our lives. We should be glad when another prospers knowing that whatever is possible for another is also possible for us. The Perfect Power within does not play favorites. Whatever we can accept for ourselves and confidently expect is going to become our experience.

The Prosperity Solution

Money is Love in action. Love and money go hand in hand. I rejoice in your good. I am glad you have plenty. May God bless all that you have and all that you share and cause you to prosper abundantly.

Pitfall Number Ten:

Accepting poverty as one's destiny.

And, finally, a pitfall that should not be overlooked is the belief that it is one's destiny to be poor and that there is nothing that can be done about it — the fatalistic attitude of blaming poverty on circumstances, race, creed, background, lack of education, etc.

Fortunately, creativity is not limited by past circumstances. A study of the biographies of successful men and women points up the fact that more often than not these people emerged from humble beginnings. Many of our great financiers were immigrants who could not even speak the English language when they arrived on our shores. Today we make it compulsory for our young people to attend high school, and yet, I know hundreds of people who reached great heights without even a high school education. They are proud of the fact that they are completely self-educated. What do these people who succeeded and prospered after overcoming great odds have in common? All had the desire to succeed coupled with determination, perseverance, a willingness to keep on in spite of repeated failure, and were not afraid of hard work.

The Prosperity Solution

I choose to look at my assets instead of my liabilities. Nothing can interfere with the perfect right action of God Almighty within me. I refuse to be governed by the past. Circumstances have no power over me. I am opening the way for right action to express in and through my life now.

Did any of these pitfalls sound familiar to you? If you feel that you relate even a little bit to any of them, I advise you to overcome them. The dictionary defines the word *pitfall* as: *a trap made by digging a hole in the ground and concealing its opening; any danger or difficulty that is not easily anticipated or avoided.* We certainly don't want you stumbling into any of these "concealed holes" as you build your prosperity consciousness. Take time to fill them with good, constructive thoughts and you will not be trapped by them in the future.

Remember, your word for good renders successful everything that you undertake. Expect success and you will find success. Your feeling of inner wealth will neutralize any suggestion of lack on the outside. The infinite Abundance is your abundance. It flows through Mind into manifestation. Know that God gives you the necessary ideas and clothes them with all that is needed to bring them into form. Cease struggling with the outside conditions and turn now to the infinite Source within. The floodgates are now opened and good is poured forth into your experience. Think prosperity. Speak prosperity. Dare to give freely and receive freely. You cannot outgive God.

Self-Direction

Declare with assurance: *I am prosperity. I think prosperity. I speak prosperity. My every act produces prosperity.*

I dare to give freely knowing that I cannot outgive God.

As I think prosperity I demonstrate prosperity. I am no longer afraid to accept my good.

I know that nothing can be taken away from me that is mine by right of consciousness.

That which I can conceive of, believe in and confidently expect is going to become my experience.

And so it is.

Chapter V

"BE YE TRANSFORMED BY THE RENEWING OF YOUR MIND"

During the more than twenty years that I was actively engaged in one-to-one counseling I discovered that most of the people came because they felt they were not succeeding in life; *each one had, in some way, underrated himself and his capacity to succeed in life; each one had failed to direct his own mind into right avenues that would bring him fulfillment; each one thought that life was against him when the truth was, he was against himself.*

I discovered that there was a law of mind that worked in every instance if the person involved was willing to give it a try. Whenever a person was willing to change his thinking, giving new conscious direction to his subconscious mind, there was an immediate change in his outer experience. [1]

In this chapter we are going to discuss some of the ways that we can give new direction to the subconscious mind so that it will work with us in our quest for prosperity.

[1]Jack Ensign Addington, PSYCHOGENESIS, Everything Begins In Mind (Dodd, Mead & Co., 1971)

Perhaps you are thinking that you are going to have to change your conditions before you can attain a prosperity state of mind; that you are going to have to manipulate life in some way to change your conditions. I have news for you. The place to start is with your thinking. *Everything begins in mind*, your mind, for it is the thoughts that you entertain that produce your world.

Human beings are continually feeding ideas into their subconscious minds, ideas they *don't* want to experience.

Suppose you have a pail of dirty water and you keep pouring clean water into it; eventually you are going to have a pail of clean water. The subconscious mind can be compared to a pail of dirty water. What we need to do is pour enough clean water (constructive ideas) into it to cleanse it. Then it will go to work for us to produce success and prosperity.

Since we are, each one of us, a part of the Universal Subconscious Mind, this has far-reaching consequences whereby we are able to draw to us the ways and means of our prosperity until all of life is working with us.

> *. . . the action of thought-power is not limited to a circumscribed individuality.*
> *What the individual does is to give direction to something which is unlimited, to call into action a force infinitely greater than his own,*

which because it is in itself impersonal though intelligent, will receive the impress of his personality, and can therefore make its influence felt far beyond the limits which bound the individual's objective perception of the circumstances with which he has to deal.

—Thomas Troward, Edinburgh Lectures

Self-Direction Is The Way To Go

Self-Direction is the art of directing the subconscious mind into channels of right use. There is no longer any doubt in my mind about the effectiveness of this approach. *That which a person believes about himself, and which he confidently expects, will become his experience.*

Whereas we have, in the past, given negative direction to the subconscious mind, we are going to start now giving constructive direction to it. There are various ways to do this. In this chapter we are going to consider a few of them.

But, before we do, I'd like to say that too many people take themselves too seriously. They consider that it is their bounden duty to worry about life, to stew about situations in life, to impress others with their negative thinking. They feel that out of loyalty to themselves and their fellow man they must prove up their negative thinking. It is obvious, then, that before we embark on this new constructive thinking program we must take a right-about-face, if we are the negative type, and kick the old thinking out the door and refuse to let it back in.

Affirmations—Their Value And Why They Work

Affirmations are positive, constructive statements phrased in the first person. They are used in order to establish in the individual a new order of thinking. Sometimes we precede the affirmation with a denial of the old order of thinking. Here are some affirmations you will be using:

I am prosperity, I think prosperity, I live prosperity.
Everything I do prospers.
I put no limit upon my supply for it comes to me from an infinite Source.
I refuse to identify with hard times. I am in business with God and God's business is good.

The idea is to use these affirmations over and over, repeat them aloud if it helps you, until you are able to believe them. There is nothing superstitious about this. It is not a hocus-pocus, voodoo chant. There is no efficacy in repeating the affirmations by rote out of superstition. You have to feel them and accept them in order for them to be effective.

Yes, I know, you're going to feel silly at first saying, "I am prosperity," with that pile of unpaid bills in front of you. It takes salesmanship. You're going to have to *sell yourself* on the idea that there is a new order of thinking for you and then it will become your experience.

Try Using a Seven-Day Mental Diet as a Beginning

Just as it is important to consistently take in the right kinds of food in order that our bodies function well, so it is important to establish a pattern of consistently ingesting the right kind of thoughts. There is nothing like using a seven-day mental diet to get started on your new thought training program. Here is one you can use:

A Seven-Day Mental Diet for Prosperity

The over-all idea for this mental diet is going to be: I AM PROSPERITY. This means that right within you is all that you will ever need to bring about prosperity—the wisdom, the intelligence, the power, the ideas, everything you need begins in your mind.

The way to use this mental diet is that each day you will once each hour repeat with feeling the affirmation for that day. By the end of the day we hope you will have *digested it*. In other words, as with using any affirmation, through repetition you will make it yours. This is a mind training exercise that has been found to be very effective.

1st day: *My success does not depend upon outer conditions. I AM PROS-PERITY.*

2nd day: *I am letting go of old limiting ideas and replacing them with thoughts of success and divine right action. I AM PROSPERITY.*

3rd day: *I refuse to dwell upon lack. I am prospered in all that I do. I AM PROSPERITY.*

4th day: *I am one with the lavish abundance of the universe forever expanding. I AM PROSPERITY.*

5th day: *New opportunities open up to me just as I need them. I AM PROSPERITY.*

6th day: *I am demonstrating prosperity because there is nothing in me to deny it. I AM PROSPERITY.*

7th day: *I receive my good gladly, allowing others to prosper in the joy of giving. I AM PROSPERITY.*

Meditation as a Means
of Mind-Cleansing

Meditation puts us in tune with Life and when we are in tune with Life all of Life works with us. I have used a capitol "L" here because I am referring to the Universal which knows no limitation. Try starting your day with a fifteen minute meditation. To begin with, take one of the positive affirmations I have given you and mentally live with it. Let it expand in your mind. For instance, take the idea: *I am one with Life and Life is one with me. All of Life is working with me to bring about my prosperity.* Feel your oneness with Life. God loves you and wants you to be happy and fulfilled in all that you do. When you prosper, you prosper to the glory of God. Nothing can separate you from your good. Meditate on these ideas and you will come away from your meditation with a new feeling about Life and your relationship to it.

Repeat this program each day and you will make real progress in your mind-training program.

Statement of Truth Cards Can Be a Great Help

Every year through the magazine, Abundant Living, we offer a Prosperity Program to help people build a prosperity consciousness. We offer various affirmations each year on wallet size cards that can easily be carried with the student during the day to facilitate using them often. We call these Statement of Truth cards. Do you remember when you were

in the primary grades and your teacher held up
"flash cards" to help you picture in your mind the
words and phonics that you were to use that day?
In my school we learned our arithmetic combina-
tions in the same way. We looked at $6 + 4 = 10$
so many times that finally it stuck in our minds. In
this way we learned to add and multiply and this
knowledge stayed with us through life. Repetition
is the key. You can make yourself "flash cards" by
copying down the affirmations we will give you at
the end of each Chapter. Use them often during the
day and you will make them yours forever.

Treatments Are for Specific Overcoming

From time to time, we will be giving you mental
treatments which you can use for the purpose of
changing the mind in some specific area. For instance, suppose you are unemployed and you would
like to change your mind to a consciousness of being rightly employed. Here is a "treatment" that
you can use:

I Am Always Rightfully Employed

I do not accept unemployment or lack of
employment in my experience. I am always in the
right place at the right time doing the right
things. I am always employed in doing creative
work that is right and perfect for my talents.
I am always receiving right and perfect remuneration. I am happy in my work.

God is my employer and God rewards my service
with generous remuneration and lavish praise. For
this I give thanks.

And so it is

Self-Direction for a Prosperity State of Mind

My supply is from God; my good is of God.
It may seem to come through man; but it is not
    from man.
God gives to me in many ways.
God gives to me according to my acceptance of
    the Infinite.
I depend upon God and I am never disappointed.
    "If God be for me, who can be against me."

And so it is.

Chapter VI

PREPARING THE WAY
FOR PROSPERITY

The other day I had lunch with a man who has had a rather unique record of success in business. I asked him, "To what do you attribute your continual prosperity?"

He laughed and scratched his head and then he said, "Well, I guess I just think things through before I do them."

"Doesn't everybody?" I countered.

"Maybe," he replied, "but most of them think the things through negatively and that's the reason they fail."

His approach excited me and I questioned him further.

"Well, I suppose I picture it all in my mind," he went on, "Sort of like going to a play. I visualize each step and see myself succeeding. In my thinking, there's no place for failure. If things don't seem to be working out, I take another tack, but, always, in my mind, I see the end result as working out successfully. I guess you'd say that I'm a confirmed winner, not a loser."

The Proper Use of Creative Imagination

Everyone of us is endowed with the faculty of creative imagination. You notice I say *creative* imagination. Creative imagination is using the imagination creatively to envision that which we desire. We all use the mental faculty called imagination, but sometimes we use it erroneously, picturing in our minds situations that we really do not want to experience. Everything that happens to us is created in the invisible world of the mind.

You see, it behooves us if we would be happy, to understand something about creative imagination. Otherwise, we may be planting mental seeds we do not want to harvest. As Job said, *The thing I greatly feared has come to pass.*

Creative Imagination Goes Before Us
And Prepares the Way

Creative imagination is a form of prayer. Jesus was speaking of creative imagination when he said, *What things soever ye desire, when ye pray, believe that ye receive them, and ye shall have them.* In other words, if you can imagine receiving your desires, they will come into your experience.

The farmer uses creative imagination as it was intended to be used. When he plants the corn he has in mind the full-grown corn stalk, the ears filled with corn. He envisions the time of harvest. Those who have succeeded in life have invariably used creative imagination properly. Tschaikovsky had a complete symphony in mind before he ever sat down to write it.

Using Creative Imagination in Selling

A salesman plans to make a call in the morning. It is a very important call to him. If he is a successful salesman he does not weary himself by wondering what kind of a negative answer he is going to receive. Instead, he pictures in his mind the successful sale. He imagines himself confidently meeting the customer, presenting his ideas and closing the sale. Using creative imagination he is able to anticipate his customer's questions. When he actually makes his sales presentation he is poised and confident. The customer also feels relaxed and the sale is successfully concluded.

One time a real estate salesman came to me. He told me that he had had a very poor year. "I have put many, many sales into escrow but they all fell through," he said.

I asked him, "What do you picture in your mind when you are showing people the property?"

"Oh," he said, "I picture the sale in escrow."

"Well," I said, "it surely is working for you. They all go into escrow and that's as far as they get. Now let's start picturing the completed sale, the money distributed, the buyer happy, and you happy. Start visualizing the completed sale."

"I never thought of that," he said. But once he tried creative imagination, the whole picture changed.

In the same way we are all creating our heaven and earth through our inner beliefs about ourselves. So let's give thanks for the wonder and glory of the Perfect Power within, realizing that we are given tools to use. Creative imagination is one of the most wonderful tools of all when we use it rightly.

The Way Creative Imagination Works

We have seen that creative imagination works, bringing into manifestation our negative thoughts as well as our constructive thinking. I think that Dr. Ernest Holmes explained the use of the imagination better than anyone:

> *Just imagine yourself surrounded by Mind, so plastic, so receptive, that it receives the slightest impression of your thought. Whatever you think, it takes up and executes for you. Every thought is received and acted upon. Not some, but all thoughts. Whatever the pattern we provide, that will be our demonstration. If we cannot get over thinking we are poor, then we will remain poor. As soon as we become rich in our thought, then we will be rich in our expression. These are not mere words, but the deepest truth that has ever come to the human race. Hundreds of thousands of the most intelligent thinkers and the most spiritual people of our day are proving this truth. We are not dealing with illusions but with realities; pay no more attention to the one who ridicules these*

ideas than you would to the blowing of the wind. In the center of your own soul choose what you want to become, to accomplish; then keep it to yourself. Every day in the silence of absolute conviction KNOW that it is done. For, it is just as much done, as far as you are concerned, as it will be when you experience it in the outer. Imagine yourself to be what you want to be. See only that which you desire, refuse even to think of the other. Stick to it, never doubt. Say many times a day, "I am that thing," and realize what this means. For it means that the great Universal power of Mind IS that, and it CANNOT FAIL. [1]

Opportunity Never Stops Knocking

Moaning and groaning about missed opportunities is such a futile waste of time. Human judgment leads to misinterpretation of so many events in life. "It could have been — if only I had of — I missed my chance, etc., etc.," are traps for those who allow themselves to get caught up in living in the past. Today's opportunities are just as fruitful and productive as the opportunities of yesterday. Creativity is eternal. Opportunity keeps right on knocking on our door. It's never too late. Ideas keep coming unless we close them off, and these ideas can turn into prosperity goals achieved.

[1] Ernest S. Holmes, CREATIVE MIND AND SUCCESS (Dodd, Mead & Co., 1947)

Doing First Things First

The other day I read an article in the newspaper about a man who was the head of a large business. His friends were celebrating his 90th birthday by having a big party for him. He was still active and creative in his business. His friends told him not to expect another such birthday party for another 90 years. This active, creative man remarked that his business premise was to always put first things first. He felt that many people wasted their time, effort and energy on matters that could just as well be left undone. "Do the most important thing first," was his advice, "and you will always be doing the most important thing."

I couldn't help but think as I read the story that moaning and whining about lost opportunities is not putting first things first. Every moment we spend looking backward with regret is a moment wasted that could be spent on today's opportunities.

Act As Though You Are and You Will Be

Before a person can prosper he has to think of himself as prosperous. It helps to claim prosperity for yourself. Affirm daily:

I AM PROSPEROUS.
EVERYTHING I DO PROSPERS.
I GIVE TO LIFE AND LIFE GIVES
BACK TO ME.

Act as though you are and you will be. This does not mean to go out and run up a lot of debts, nor pretend that you are something that you aren't. It means to set your goals and start thinking of yourself as achieving them.

The little girl who dresses up like mother and pretends her dolls are children is laying the foundation for being a good mother. The young people who work in Junior Achievement, forming a corporation, conceiving and developing a product, producing and selling that product and keeping the books, doing all of the things done by a successful business, are laying the foundation for being successful business people and will become real achievers.

The great Goethe wrote these famous lines:

Are you in earnest? Seize this very minute;
What you can do or dream you can do, begin
it. Boldness has genius, power and magic in it.
Only engage and the mind becomes heated.
Begin, and the work will be completed.

Another power-filled thought is: *Do the thing and you will have the power.* Ralph Waldo Emerson said that. I go back to this thought often in my work. It seems as if my wife and I are always biting off more than we can chew. But, whenever I feel stalled and unable to accomplish, I just step in and start doing it. The trip begins with the first step. Lo, and behold, the work gets done. My wife and I dreamed of writing many books. They don't write themselves. It takes a lot of work. But one step at a time, we have plugged along, the dream always foremost in our minds. You know the rest. Today, we have quite a list of published books. Yes, *act as though you are and you will be*.

Self-Direction

I am prosperous. (Think this over a hundred times, if you have to, until it becomes embedded in your subconscious.) I never entertain thoughts of poverty or lack.

I am supplied from the Infinite Source with all that I need and to spare.

Right ideas come to me when I need them. I make right decisions at the right time.

I am never alone. I have a Silent Partner who works with me in everything that I do. He is right within me, working with me every moment of the day.

I have no regrets for the past, no fear for this moment, nor any anxiety for the future. I am protected by an Infinite Power; I am guided by Divine Intelligence and I am sustained by a Loving Presence.

All is well and I am thankful.

                                        And so it is.

Chapter VII

HOW THE LAWS OF LIFE
CAN WORK FOR YOU

We live in a universe of law and order. There are definite laws that apply to every activity in life. They will work for us or against us depending upon how we use them. We live in a mental world and therefore it is very important that we understand certain mental laws. The laws of life are impersonal. They do not care how we use them. Fortunately for us, we have been given the power of choice. These wonderful laws are here for us to use. It is up to us how we use them.

The Law of Identification

The first law we are going to consider is the law of identification. It simply means: *whatever you identify yourself with, you become*. Talking "poor mouth" as they say down south, can make you poor. Talking opulence, on the other hand, can help you to be rich.

Words, words, words! Millions of words are written and spoken every day. Some we think are important and some are more important to us than we realize.

I was talking one day to a man from the People's Republic of China who was in the United States to study the computer sciences. "How do you manage in China", I asked him, "when you do not have words in your vocabulary covering the computer language or the field of electronics?"

"Yes," he said, "we do not have a Chinese vocabulary that we can use, so we use English words."

Not only are words important from a technical point of view, but they have a tremendous impact on our personal lives, for words are fraught with emotion. Words engender feelings that affect the mind, body and experience of the person using them.

Jesus understood this. He said: *By thy words thou shalt be justified and by thy words thou shalt be condemned.* It is very important that we understand which words will prosper us and which words will condemn us to poverty.

There are prosperity words and there are poverty words. Let's try some prosperity words and see how they make us feel. How about *opulent; affluent; enriching; plenteous; flourishing and abundant?* How about saying these words over a few times just to see how you feel.

Now let's identify with these words in an affirmation and see what they will do for us:

I am opulent in the abundance of life. Every moment of my life is an enriching experience. I see abundance everywhere. The seeds of prosperity planted in my mind are plenteous and flourishing. I am affluent. All that the Father hath is mine.

How about *triumphant* as a prosperity word? *I am triumphant over negative and destructive thinking.*

One time I heard a woman referred to as *a radiant soul.* I looked forward to meeting her and, sure enough, when I met her, I saw what her admirers meant. She was *a radiant soul.* She was an enlightened person who really let her light shine. She prospered in everything that she did because life agreed with her and she agreed with life.

Let's look at a few more prosperity words: *exuberant* means *to be abundant; to be fruitful.* Its synonyms are: *abundant; plenteous; effusive; lavish; overflowing and profuse. To exuberate,* the dictionary tells us is *to abound.*

Another great word is *copious.* It is another word for *abundance, to abound in* and its synonyms are: *profuse; plentiful; abundant; ample; rich; full; overflowing.*

There is no end to these prosperous words: *proficient; expansive; enthusiastic; inspiring; powerful; commanding; dynamic; potent; capable; competent; profuse; luxuriant; prime; superb.* All of these are constructive words, words that will build your consciousness of prosperity. Say them aloud and identify yourself with each word by putting "I am" in front of it. Feel the power behind the word as you identify yourself with it. Remember: *there is a law of life that whatever you identify yourself with, you become.* This is a feeling thing that sinks deep into your subconscious mind. Feeling gives rise to action. If you don't believe me, try saying *I feel wonderful,* slowly and with feeling three times. Don't you feel better? You will find this is a good way to dispel the blues or rout depression. Of course, you must say it with feeling *and believe it*, paying no attention to conditions or circumstances.

Now try saying *I am prosperous! Everything I do prospers.* Say it over and over with the same feeling. Believe it. It will go to work for you. You will never be the same again.

To really understand the negative use of the law of identification we're going to have to take a look at some poverty words. You need not strike these words from your vocabulary but make yourself a solemn vow never to allow them to be identified with you. It is equally important not to use them in connection with another. You do an injustice to another when you identify that person with any of these words and some of it is bound to rub off on you. Here are some poverty words to avoid: *poor; sad; lacking; anxious; hopeless; indolent; deprived; dismal; scant; underprivileged; oppressed; de-*

pressed. Just a few. I could go on and make the list much longer but I dislike working with poverty words. I like prosperity words better, don't you?

Some people seem to think that they are being compassionate when they associate poverty words with another. This is not true. It is a form of condemnation. Each person is a creative, expressive being who needs to be recognized as such. Everyone desires to feel important to life, to contribute something to life and each is endowed with something to contribute. We all need love which is expressed through respect and good will. Prosperity words help to express love and understanding. Whenever we think prosperity for another we are also accepting prosperity for ourselves and both will benefit.

Whatever we bring into the lives of others, comes back into our own. Was there ever a better time to think prosperity for ourselves and the world that we may all prosper to the glory of God!

The Law of Attraction

As fish dwell in the sea, so do we *live and move and have our being* in a sea of mind. If we can think of it as a plastic, fluidic substance which is always ready to respond to us, we would be better able to understand the law of attraction. We are like magnets which draw to us that which our thoughts embody. We draw into our experience that which we believe and accept for ourselves.

We live in mind, wrote Ernest Holmes, *and It can return to us only what we think into It. No matter what we do, Law will always obtain. If we are thinking of ourselves as poor and needy, then Mind has no choice but to return what we have thought into It. "It is done unto you as you believe." Thoughts of failure, limitation or poverty are negative and must be counted out of our lives for all time. God has given us a Power and we must use It. We can do more toward saving the world by proving this law than all that charity has ever given to it.*

Do you see now why it is so important to identify with opulent words? Why we dare not let fear of poverty dominate our thinking? Remember what happened to Job that caused him to say, *What I greatly feared has come to pass.* Job had everything taken away from him and wound up sitting among the ashes, covered with boils from the soles of his feet to the top of his head, scratching himself with a piece of broken pottery. After that I'll bet he watched his thoughts lest what he greatly feared should come upon him again.

Job had used the law of attraction in reverse, but we're going to see how we can use it affirmatively and constructively.

JOY IS AN INSIDE JOB wrote Don Blanding and used it for the title of one of his best books. As Jesus prefaced so many of his great truths with the words, *verily, verily I say unto thee*, (which means *truly, truly I tell you*), truly, truly I tell you *pros-*

perity is an inside job. There is only one place to create it and that is in consciousness. The outer will always follow as effect always follows cause. Therefore, if we do not like our present circumstances, we should leave off struggling with them and start building a consciousness of true prosperity, a feeling of inner security which is eternal (unchanging) wealth. This is the master key to prosperity. Ultimately, it will be to you like having the goose that lays golden eggs or a money tree in the back yard; but, you must seek spiritual security for its own sake and prosperity will follow.

So often people evaluate their prosperity according to prestige symbols, such as great possessions or high position. These are only the by-products of consciousness. They are here today and gone tomorrow. That is why so many achieve great wealth oftentimes only to lose it. Others recoup their losses and make one fortune after another.

The only true and lasting prosperity is that which is founded solidly on the rock of Truth. This is what Jesus meant when he said, *For he that hath, to him shall be given: and he that hath not, from him shall be taken even that which he hath.* We might paraphrase this statement to make it still clearer: For he that has a consciousness of true wealth shall be given wealth, and he that has a consciousness of lack and poverty will lose even that which he had. Is it not clear, then, that a person who has great possessions and starts worrying about how to hang onto them, how to keep from losing that which he has stored up in the outer, soon develops a consciousness of lack and his outer affairs just as quickly mirror this change in consciousness? It is plain to see that whatever contributes to our inner awareness of wealth contributes to our outer expression of wealth. As Jesus said again, *thy Father which seeth in secret shall reward thee openly.*

Prosperity is not an impossible dream; it is not a "castle in the sky," not a continual diet of thick steaks and rich desserts. Prosperity is an inward feeling that whatever we attempt is already being accomplished; whatever we desire is being manifested; whatever our goal, it is attained. Prosperity is a feeling that life is working with us, that we are working with life and enjoying it.

The Law of Cause and Effect

We live in a mental world. Do you believe this? That which appears is made out of the invisible Substance of Life. We mold this fluidic Substance by our thoughts. No one limits our thoughts but ourselves. No one directs our thoughts but ourselves. Each person has the choice and can decide what kind of world he is going to live in and the direction that his life shall take. Life is an individual experience; therefore, what one selects for himself becomes his experience. We cannot make the experience of another because it is impossible to get into the consciousness of another. Brainwashing is a temporary thing and very unsatisfactory at best.

So, I ask you: What do you think about yourself? What do you think about your world? What do you think about others? Do you resent the success of others? If you do, you are condemning yourself to failure. Are you expanding your consciousness or contracting it? Do you believe in prosperity, or are you a poverty worshiper? It is up to you to choose.

What do you think of your world? Do you love it, or do you hate it? Do you agree with it, or do you resist it? Do you take it for granted? Or, are you aware of it as the wonderful expression of life itself?

What do you think of others? Do you judge other people and find yourself constantly comparing yourself to them? Are you willing to see others suc-ceed? Are you able to get rid of that old "devil," jealousy? Do you resent the success of others? If you do, you are condemning yourself to failure, for failure is where your attention is focused.

Do you see that prosperity depends upon you and you alone? If you are not now prosperous, it will take a change of consciousness on your part. For every cause there is an effect and for every effect there is a cause.

The Law of Increase

If a person would sit still each morning for even 15 minutes and bless his business, invoking the Law of Increase in that business, he would find his business would really start to prosper. The Law of Increase will go to work and bring increase to that firm. That to which we give our attention is bound to increase. People will be attracted to what the business has to sell, no matter whether it is a service or a product and all things will work together for good for that business. It is a matter of accepting our good right where we are, being optimists instead of pessimists, looking to the optimum good instead of to lack. This is investing in prosperity.

If your business seems to be slack, try thinking about giving rather than getting. Invest in service and let the chips fall where they may. You cannot outgive God. Whatever you give into life will surely return to you.

In our next chapter we will see how different people have successfully applied the law of giving and receiving in their lives.

Self Direction

There is no power in lack. There is no power in poverty. There is no power in adverse circumstances or conditions.

There is only one power, the Perfect Power within. Through a recognition of this truth, I am transmuting all thoughts of lack into a realization of divine abundance in my life.

All of the Intelligence and Power of God is expressing in and through me. My every need is met.

I cease looking at lack and my whole attention is directed to that which is real and perfect.
I deny the lie of lack and affirm the truth of divine Abundance.

And so it is.

Chapter VIII

THE LAW OF GIVING
AND RECEIVING

Where prosperity is concerned, the most important law of life for us to understand is the law of giving and receiving. In the Bible it is called sowing and reaping. It is based on the circulatory activity of life. All of life is in continual circulation. If we do not give back into life we interfere with and eventually dam up the circulatory activity.

The person who gives of himself and his substance, no matter how little, opens the door for life to pour in, not only compensating him for his gift, but increasing the gift. The more one gives the more that person is able to receive.

Many Business People Have Discovered That Giving Is Receiving

Have you ever wondered why it is that some people seem to have such phenomenal success, outdistancing everyone else in their field? A highly successful insurance salesman once gave the key to his success. His name was Vash Young. He wrote a best-seller about it entitled A FORTUNE TO SHARE. The man was tops in his field. He won most of the prizes offered by his company. Year after year he made the million dollar round table. The rest of the salesmen considered him lucky, but there was no doubt in their minds that he was the most successful man in the company.

But was it luck? His book revealed the secret. He carried around in his billfold a very dog-eared index card, yellow with age on which he had written the verse. It was Luke 6:38.

> *Give and it shall be given unto you; good measure, pressed down, and shaken together, and running over, shall men give into your bosom. For with the same measure that ye mete withal it shall be measured to you again.*

He said that up to the time that he had discovered this verse in the Bible, he had been considered a go-getter. He made sales all right. He closed them by whatever means he could. However, his high-pressure methods made him very few friends. And then, he came across that verse in Luke. He said it stood out as if a bright light had been focused upon it.

The next day he went out with an entirely different attitude. He determined to see how much service he could give away.

"I decided I would be a go-giver instead of a go-getter!" he said.

And then, the whole picture changed. He stopped thinking about "how am I doing and what am I going to get out of this," and life took care of him in wonderful ways. You see, it is a law of life: *The more you give away, the more you keep.*

> *There was a man and they called him mad*
> *The more he gave, the more he had.*
> —John Bunyan

My wife and I had two friends whom we admired very much. They have both passed on but I feel sure they would not have minded my telling you this story about them. They were maiden ladies who were very successful in real estate, delightfully Irish with a great sense of humor. Good Catholics, both of them, they once told me that whenever business became slack they decided it was time to give a little more. So, they would write out a generous check. I think it was to The Little Sisters of the Poor. I'm sure they did not do this just to make money for they were very giving people. They told me about it because they knew I understood and as we talked they fairly glowed with the joy it gave them to give that extra tithe to the church charity of their choice.

Everybody in town knew these two ladies and loved them. It was only natural that they got plenty of referrals. They were givers, not getters, but life always gave back to them even more than they gave.

Giving Is Receiving

A man befriended an elderly woman who lived alone. He, too, had no thought of personal gain as he went out of his way to do little things for a lonely woman. He visited her frequently, ran errands for her, and they became good friends. She told him that although she had grown children of her own, she felt closer to him than she did to her own children. Knowing that she was lonely, he stopped by often to see her. One day as they sat in her living room visiting, he happened to remark that he had become very interested in art.

"There are a number of paintings in my attic," she told him. "Perhaps you'd be interested in some of them."

As he started up the attic steps, she called after him, "If there are any paintings that interest you, bring them down. Pick out the ones you like and you are welcome to have them."

The attic hadn't had a visitor for many years. Nothing had been disturbed judging by the thick layer of dust on everything. He had gone up to the attic wearing a dark blue suit. It was a charcoal grey when he came down. But soon the clouds of dust were forgotten as he began to examine the paintings. Here was a collector's dream come true. Imagine his excitement as he discovered that several of the paintings were by well-known artists and would be considered quite valuable. He could tell that they were genuine, paintings that had been out of circulation for years, hidden away in this dusty attic. His excitement grew as he uncovered painting after painting that would create a sensation in an art auction. Hurrying downstairs, he explained to his elderly friend that she had a fortune in paintings in her attic.

"Allow me to have them appraised," he offered. "I will be glad to pay you every cent they are worth."

"I should say not," the little woman told him. "I had forgotten that they were there, and so they are of little value to me. Take all that you want. It is my great pleasure to give them to you."

To her, the paintings had little value. She had no need of money but friendship freely given to a lonely old woman was of great value. How happy she was to be able to do something for him!

Give and it shall be given unto you, pressed down, shaken together and running over shall men give unto your bosom, said the Master who understood better than anyone else the laws of life.

That Which We Give Into the Lives of Others Comes Back Into Our Own

The man who told me the story of the long lost paintings added a story of his own. "It's not much of a story," he said, "but in a way it has similar meaning."

"I left home at sixteen," he said. "Life at home had become intolerable and I discovered that if I had a job and a place to stay, I would be allowed to leave home. I found myself a job working in a restaurant. At first I lived in my car, but then a friend introduced me to a woman who had a big house. This woman needed a boy to do the gardening, and I offered to do this in exchange for the privilege of sleeping in a room that she did not use.

"At first," he said, "I just slept in the room and continued to study in the car, but gradually we talked together more and more. She took an interest in my welfare, and began very delicately to advise me and to look out for me. She was lonely and so was I. I soon discovered that she wasn't eating properly. The cook at the restaurant began to give me leftovers that he couldn't use. Sometimes he gave me a half of a chicken, or a part of a roast. There was more than I could eat and so I brought the food home to her. It seemed quite natural sharing our meals, each one looking out for the other. I was so glad to be able to see that she ate regular meals, and I suppose she felt the same way about me."

And so began a wonderful relationship, two lonely people helping each other. The boy continued to live there until he finished school, his life enriched by this gentle woman who helped him find himself without seeming to interfere with his freedom. She had found a son and he had found the roots he badly needed at that time. He smiled tenderly as he remembered again those days. "I'm a bad one for remembering birthdays and anniversaries," he said, "but I had my wife write down the special days in the life of this woman and together we never forget her."

> *There is a destiny that makes us brothers;*
>   *No man goes his way alone;*
> *All that we send into the lives of others*
>   *Comes back into our own.*
> —Edwin Markham

I think these stories pretty much speak for themselves. Now contrast them with this one.

Using the Law in Reverse

Mr. Puddy and Julie are two of the characters who lived at 10 Dulcimer Street, London, in Norman Collins' story, LONDON BELONGS TO ME. Mr. Puddy lived in the attic. He was a widower, a morose, fat man, often changing jobs and delighting in eating. Julie was an old lady who lived in a room at the back of the second floor of the house, and worked in the cloakroom of a night club. Returning from work, Julie was involved in a traffic accident. She wasn't seriously hurt, but Mr. Puddy persuaded her to go to a solicitor and make a claim. To her great surprise, she later was paid sixty-five pounds. Remembering that but for Mr. Puddy she would never have received a penny, she felt she ought to give him half the amount. This could not be immediately done since the money was in the form of a check.

Later she decided that since she, and not Mr. Puddy, had been involved in the accident, a fourth would be enough to give him. The thought of fifteen crisp pound notes caused her to hesitate again. In any case, was it proper for a lady to give money to a man? A better idea would be to buy him a present — say a pair of cufflinks.

Back in her room, Julie felt a twinge of pain. Perhaps it was an indication of something seriously wrong with her, and if so, she would need all of her sixty-five pounds. A happy idea came to her. She would give Mr. Puddy a tin of soup for his supper. Better still, she would make it herself and take it to him in a bowl on a tray. When she reached for the tin of soup, she found that by adding water one tin could be made sufficient for two people. So she prepared half of the tin of soup for Mr. Puddy and took it to him to show her gratitude for his help. Thus, a little over thirty-two pounds became a half a tin of thin soup.

Don't laugh. I suppose we've all been guilty of having some generous impulse rationalized by us into the equivalent of a half a tin of thin soup. It's so easy to talk ourselves out of our good inspiration along giving lines. Yes, *give and it shall be given unto you; good measure, pressed down, and shaken together, and running over*, is the law; but the Master added: *For with the same measure that ye mete withal it shall be measured to you again.* Another time he said: *Freely ye have received, freely give.*

Halford E. Luccock in LIVING WITHOUT GLOVES wrote:

> *It is more blessed to give than to receive. But the givers who cannot take in return miss one of the finest graces in life, the grace of receiving. To receive gratefully from others is to enhance others' sense of their worth. It puts them on a give-and-take level, the only level on which real fellowship can be sustained. It changes one of the ugliest things in the world, patronage, into one of the richest things in the world, friendship.*

The Law at Work

The law is that we must first give before we are able to receive. Just as the seed must first be planted before the fruit can appear, so must we plant generously if we would reap generously. He who gives meagerly, or for what he can gain from the gift, receives but meagerly. Ah, but he who would give freely, with no thought of gain, is going to receive richly. You can't outgive God!

As someone once said, "You make a living with what you get, but you make a life with what you give."

We're talking about a law of life. Giving is not just parting with something, it is opening the heart and mind to receive again from Life's infinite storehouse. We find that the more we give the more we are able to receive.

Some of you may remember the old-fashioned pump. Remember how we used to have to take the dipper and pour a little water down into the pump to get the flow started? This was known as "priming the pump," and the pump refused to give water until it was "primed." This is pretty much the way it is all through life. We have to give first and then life will give unto us, yes, *pressed down, shaken together and running over.*

I have known many people in my life who have prospered greatly because they learned the law of giving and receiving and put it into practice. Today these people are well provided for because they dared to give themselves away, dared to give that which they had and sometimes even more than they thought they had at the time. They gave freely with no thought of reward, and then, when they had even forgotten the gifts they had given, in came the harvest of life bringing them the increase — all that they needed and many times more.

Prosperous People Are Good Receivers

The prosperous people I know are good receivers. They have learned to accept their good and be grateful for it.

Over and over people write me: "Please tell me how to receive." It occurs to me that one simple approach might be to start saying "thank you" to life. Thank God for your food, no matter who prepares it. Thank God for the air you breathe, the services that are performed for you. Thank God for the things provided for you by the city, the state, the federal government. Let's turn our discontent and critical thoughts into gratitude for the good already received. Praise and bless each thing that comes our way and see what happens. We might all of us be surprised. Learning to receive starts with gratitude and appreciation for good already received.

Lots of times people are too wary to be good receivers. They are afraid that if they let someone give to them they are going to be indebted. Down south they call it "being beholden." We've got to be willing to let someone else play "lady bountiful" for awhile. The biggest givers can be niggardly when it comes to being good receivers. It takes love. It takes practice. It starts with honesty and a willingness to take a good look at ourselves. Are you denying someone else the joy of giving because you find it hard to be appreciative? If so, love demands you start learning to say "thank you."

Self-Direction

God's abundance lives through me for I am one
   with all of life.
I give freely and receive joyfully out of a consciousness of abundance.
Abundance, full measure, pressed down, shaken together, and running over is mine to use and
   to share.
Today I enter into a consciousness of abundance
   and plenty. I know that everything I do

will prosper. I expect success and I am
    successful.
I give wisely, but generously, into life. I give
    of my substance, my talents and my abilities.
As a child of God I am one with God's abundance.
    My needs are met moment by moment.

And so it is.

Chapter IX

BUILDING A CONSCIOUSNESS
OF
UNINTERRUPTED PROSPERITY

Some time back I received a letter that contained a very provocative question. Bill, father of four and breadwinner for six, wanted to know:

"How can I build a consciousness of uninterrupted prosperity?" He said his life was either feast or famine. This seemed strange, on the face of it, for he had his own real estate business and was quite successful. Still his finances gave him a lot of trouble.

"It's always feast or famine," he wrote. "One month things look so good it seems we can't miss. The next month I wonder how I'm going to make my house payment."

Bill went on to describe his financial see-saw. "When I make a couple of good deals, we live it up. Last month we bought a new car, paid cash for it out of one commission and had enough left for a vacation in Hawaii. Things really looked good. Now

I wonder what's hit me. It's always like that. What am I doing wrong?"

How To Have an Uninterrupted Prosperity Consciousness

What would you have advised Bill who had what he called "a spasmodic consciousness of prosperity," and wanted to have an uninterrupted prosperity consciousness?

I telephoned him and made two suggestions which he agreed to follow:

1. "Budget your earnings to extend over a six-month period and then live within your means. Feast-or-famine spending develops a feast-or-famine pattern. This causes one to feel poor. Putting something aside for the future tends to give one a feeling of plenty."

2. "There is something else you can do that will give you a feeling of plenty. Start a tithing program on the same basis." (Bill had been tithing off and on when he made a good commission—five percent on a lump sum. It didn't make him feel prosperous because it was hard to part with so much at one time. I suggested he follow a plan used by many other salesmen—divide his average yearly income into twelve parts and tithe by the month.)

"I'll do you one better," he replied. "I'll tithe a half tithe, five percent, on 1/12th of what I *propose* to earn this year."

"Can you honestly do this without letting it make you feel anxious?" I countered.

"Yes, I can. I make at least $50,000 in a good year. I'm going to take God's share off the top each month."

He did just that, tithing $210 a month. The interesting thing was, Bill felt rich right from the start of this new program. He was getting a big kick out of tithing this way. One day he called to tell me he was on cloud nine. He'd already made his annual quota in the first six months! He decided to up his tithe. His comment was that for selfish reasons alone he couldn't afford to tithe a half a tithe any longer. He'd decided to raise it to the traditional ten percent. This made him feel good. "I realized I wasn't just cheating God, I was limiting myself!" he said exuberantly.

"Tithing surely does change one's feeling about prosperity," was the way he put it. "I really do have a feeling of uninterrupted prosperity now. I wouldn't go back to the old hit-or-miss system for anything!" And then he added, "The best part of it all is that I am constantly being reminded each time I write my check to God's work that God is my Source — infinite abundance that never runs out."

This is why I like to teach the law of giving and receiving through regular tithing. It is a law of life that can be proved by the individual. Why does it work out that way? Because if the tithe is freely given with no ulterior motive, tithing gives the giver a feeling of abundance. It's fun to give God's money. It makes you feel rich. And when you feel rich you draw riches to you. *That which you can believe about yourself is bound to become your experience.*

Winning for God

One of our top professional golfers who had won the U.S. Open and other major tournaments had become stale. It appeared that he had lost interest in winning. About that time he joined the Mormon Church, a church that is strong on tithing. The first thing he did was start a tithing program. After that, his whole attitude changed. He remarked to a friend that it made all the difference. His old enthusiasm returned. "Now, I'm winning for God, but I'm the big winner—I get ninety percent!"

The Psychological Aspect of Tithing

I believe sincerely that a person will never be completely free in his feeling about money until he has established the habit of tithing. Without the gift to God off the top there is apt to be a subconscious fear about money. Tithing overcomes that fear because each time one tithes there is a continual recognition of the everlasting Source.

Why do I say "off the top?" I am reminded of a friend who wrote that she was borrowing the money each month to pay her tithe and wondered why paying the bills was such a struggle. Borrowing the money to pay the tithe defeats the whole purpose of tithing. If one waits until he has scraped the bottom of the barrel to give the tithe he will feel poorer than ever and the increase in consciousness and its subsequent increase in prosperity will not come.

Let us examine the psychological aspect of tithing. Why does tithing in the right way bring about such a change in the mental attitude of the tither? First and foremost, tithing is an act of faith, a proving up of one's faith. Paul said, *Now faith is the substance of things hoped for, the evidence of things not seen.* Tithing is the evidence of spiritual growth as it pertains to supply. Those who have made this growth eagerly give to the Source. When this happens the tither begins to experience the increase in the outer experience. That which he has goes farther; that which he has given returns multiplied; funds are suddenly available from completely unexpected avenues.

To prosper is to be successful in all that one undertakes. It is not just a matter of making money but of having all that one needs as he needs it. Why does this principle work so well? Because it is the law of life — that which we sow we shall also reap. To give trustingly to God's work, without thought of gain, to give with no strings attached, simply for the joy of giving, builds a consciousness of trusting in the infinite Source for our good. Because the Source is infinite, the reaping will also be infinite. Tithing is stepping out on faith and it brings *the evidence of things not seen.* Ask any tither and he or she will tell you that it comes in many surprising ways, but it comes. Tithers rarely give up tithing once they have started.

To Whom Should the Tithe Be Given?

To whom should the tithe be given? Where do you receive your spiritual inspiration? Give your tithe where you receive from the Spirit and you will be giving to God's work. Ask for guidance and guidance will come.

Some Start with a Partial Tithe

Not everyone is ready for the full tithe. This comes with spiritual growth and is usually a gradual unfoldment. Some start out with a partial tithe, sometimes only one-tenth of the ten percent usually considered tithing. Others try a quarter tithe or a third tithe, gradually working it up to a half tithe, then a full tithe. A person is able to tithe when he realizes that he simply can't outgive God. As someone has said: *We can no more keep good from coming to us if we are consciously at one with the Almighty than we can hold the tide back with our hands.* When we let life flow through us uninhibited by our fears we experience the windows of heaven opened and the blessing poured out so that there is not room enough to receive it.

True Prosperity Endures Through Thick and Thin

Tithing builds a consciousness of true prosperity. True prosperity does not depend upon outer circumstances. The prosperity state of mind is an inner state of being that endures through thick and thin.

The late Mike Todd used to say, "I have been broke many times but I've never been poor."

I like that. The person who has a consciousness of prosperity can always stage a comeback. It may seem to an observer that he doesn't win them all but in the last analysis he keeps on making progress. If he loses one job, he gets another, usually a still better position. If he loses one fortune, he makes another. And so it goes. Out of the hundreds of letters that cross my desk one theme is repeated often. The writer reports, "I didn't get the job I wrote you about, but I got one still better." Or, "That house I thought I wanted didn't work out for me, but I found another that I like much better." The person who has developed a prosperity consciousness can safely turn his desires over to the Perfect Power within. As one of the great Truth teachers used to say:

Yes, yes, Father, from Thee, unless you have something still better for me.

Prosperity is that state of mind wherein one feels secure; adequate; in harmony with life; creative and productive.

Self-Direction

As I give to God, so God gives unsparingly to me.
I tithe and I prosper in everything I do.
I give of the first-fruits of my income.
I give joyfully knowing that I cannot outgive God.
The more I give the more I receive.
I tithe and I prosper.
Richly I experience the endless supply of His Love.
I can never say "thank you" enough.

                                        And so it is.

Chapter X

HOW TO DO LESS AND
ACCOMPLISH MORE

I have in my hand a letter from a very sincere person, a woman who tells me she is working hard toward *"getting off of welfare"* which she says she has been "on" for sixteen years. I can tell by reading her letter that this woman is really trying. I feel her sincerity in every page of her letter. She has set goals for herself and has been faithfully taking the human footsteps that have come to her according to her guidance. As I read on, I can't help but wonder what can be holding her back. She tells me that she studies the Bible.

And then she gives me a very important clue as to why she has never been able to accept her good. She writes *"What I would like to know is how not to feel guilty for wanting to be prosperous and still put God first."*

Now I gather from this that she has the idea that in order to put God first she has to be poor. And that's really too bad. Whoever started the idea that there is something virtuous about poverty? And why should it have been tied to the Bible?

The Bible Is a Manual for Prosperity

The Bible is full of promises of prosperity. In fact the Master said clearly: *Seek ye first the Kingdom of God and all of these things shall be added unto you.* He'd been talking about food and clothes and the things we all need.

Your Father knoweth that ye have need of all these things. And then he said at another time, *What things soever ye desire, when ye pray, believe that ye receive them and ye shall have them.*

Jesus didn't make any distinction; nothing was ruled out. *What things soever,* could certainly include a substantial bank account, a home in the clear, good clothes and a car — whatever a person could possibly need.

I decided to look up the word "prosper" in my Bible concordance. I was amazed how many references there were. Here are a few of them:

How about this one: *They shall prosper that love thee.* That seems a small price to pay for prosperity. It amounts to keeping the first commandment, that we should love God with all our might, heart, soul and mind.

And then I find in Genesis: *That the Lord made all that Joseph did to prosper.* It seems as if everyone who sought the Lord prospered.

Here are a few more of these prosperity references: *Keep therefore the words of this covenant and do them that ye may prosper in all that ye do.*

In the Psalms we find: *And whatever he doeth shall prosper.* And here are a few more: *The God*

*of heaven, he will prosper us; . . . The Lord be
with thee and prosper thou; . . . Believe in the
Lord your God, so shall ye be established; believe
his prophets, so shall ye prosper; . . . The Lord
made him to prosper; . . . The Lord hath prospered my way.*

There are many more Bible promises concerning
prosperity. I gather it was quite a popular subject
those days, too. If you don't own a large Bible concordance, go to the library and ask to see one. Look
up the words, *prosper* and *prosperity.* The message
is loud and clear. The eternal key to prosperity is
*to seek first the Kingdom of God and continue in
partnership with God.*

It is plain to see that we are not fulfilling our
part of the contract if our attention is focused on
lack and poverty. *It is done unto you as you believe,*
was the teaching of the Master. If we believe that
life is against us; if we believe that we are destined
to be poor all of our lives, that is the way life will
work it out for us. If the woman who has been on
welfare for sixteen years believes that is all life holds
for her, she's going to go right on being on welfare.
It is a fact of life that if we believe that all of life is
working with us, and that it is the Father's good
pleasure to prosper us, wonderful new ideas will
come to us, and we shall prosper.

The Greatest Gift—The Power of Choice

God has given us the power of choice. If we
choose to serve a god of money, we will continually
fear lack. Even if we amass a fortune we will con-

tinue to feel poor for we will worry about losing it. But, if we put God first, we will be working with the Source.

I'm not suggesting that you set out to manipulate life, or use God for materialistic gain. We are not trying to make something happen. We are letting the natural tendency of life express through us. Our prayer should be: *Let Thy perfect will be done through me*. We prosper to the glory of God that we may give increasingly more to God's work. It is a partnership with God. The natural tendency of life is to multiply, reproducing itself in ever-increasing abundance.

When we put God first, we become one with His Life and the flow of good from unexpected channels sometimes comes so fast it astounds us. The key word here is *let*. *Let* it happen. *Let* your supply flow unimpeded to the glory of God. There is no virtue in being poor. I love what Emerson wrote, *We have to get our bloated nothingness out of the way of the divine circuit*.

Just imagine yourself holding a power hose. As long as there is no kink in the hose, the water pours forth. Nothing can stop the flow unless the "hose" gets twisted. It is we who put the "kinks in the hose" by our negative thinking. Our part is to keep the "kinks" out of our thinking and let the abundance pour forth.

What Is Spiritual Prosperity?

We want to reaffirm that true prosperity is a state of mind that projects itself into one's circumstances so that everything reflects this state of mind. The truly prosperous are at peace with themselves and others, at ease in all situations, free of resentment, hate and greed. Wealth is what you might call the by-product of true prosperity as is health and a general state of well-being. That which is within must always reflect out into the experience.

Spiritual prosperity must begin with absolute faith in the Source of all good to supply our needs. Our security must be an inner condition that is not affected by outer conditions. True wealth is of the Spirit.

This is why we teach tithing. Tithing is not a superstitious act designed to placate some god in the sky. It is a spiritual discipline that constantly reminds us that God *is* our supply. Tithing is putting God first. As we continually turn to the Source, trusting and knowing that *every good gift and every perfect gift is from above, and cometh down from the Father of lights, with whom is no variableness, neither shadow of turning*, we gradually overcome our fear of lack. Reports of coming recessions, depressions, the ups and downs of the stock market, etc., no longer have the power to control our thinking. Our Father is a millionaire and if we ask Him for bread He's not going to give us a stone. When we develop a trusting attitude toward the Father within, the Source of our good, something happens and our faith is rewarded. Those *good and perfect gifts* are stepped down into visible manifestation. That which we have so faithfully believed does become our experience.

Investing in True Prosperity

Developing a prosperity consciousness, an awareness of prosperity, is investing in true prosperity. When one invests in spiritual prosperity, everything else falls into place easily: the right position, the right guidance, and right action. We meet just the right people to help us, the right customers are drawn to us — all that is necessary to the manifestation of prosperity comes easily and happily when one learns to change his attitude.

Investing in prosperity is an inner experience. It does not happen overnight but is a gradual process that develops along with our spiritual enlightenment. It starts the moment a person turns to the Source, trusting and knowing that God is his supply.

How To Do Less and Do More

By this we mean: *how to accomplish more with less effort.* When we put God first, we let the divine law guide and direct our steps, we cease to exert our human efforts in what seems to be the obvious way and instead we ask for guidance and let the Creative Process direct our steps. This does not mean that we are to do nothing but that what we do is done joyously and easily in a creative way. It becomes what we might call *effortless action.* When we let the divine law express through us, we find that ideas come to us at the right time and become manifest in the outer world without stress on our part. It is the difference between living by inspiration and living by drudgery. When we *put God first* we let the Creative Process create through us. As it is said in the Bible: *Ye shall not need to fight in this battle: Set yourselves, stand ye still, and see the salvation of the Lord with you.*

The Creative Process and How It Works

That which the Spirit contemplates, it becomes—*and God said, Let there be light*. God in you is Spirit individualized. Therefore, that which you contemplate becomes the law of your being. That which you contemplate is brought forth into manifestation. The manifesting is the Creative Process at work. You do not have to do anything about it except *let go and let God* create through you. You do not make the wheat grow. You only plant the seed. In the same way, you do not build your body. The Creative Process within you builds your body, but you plant the thought seed. You do not know how to put flesh and muscle upon your bones, nor do you know how to digest your food.

Our purpose in life is to know how to live life aright. We come to see that we do this best when we stand aside a bit and let Life live through us in Its perfect way. When we become aware that God indwells us, and expresses through us in His perfect way, we are willing to let God have His perfect way with us.

You Make the Choice

Daily we are given the opportunity to make the choice: shall I fight in this battle or shall I recognize the Spirit within me as the Power and the Intelligence to perform that which is given me to do? The more we understand the Truth, the more we see that the battle really isn't our battle; that there is that within us which knows how to do everything with ease and certainty. When we let the Creative Process take place in and through us we become one with the Universe. We plant the seed in mind and all that is needed to bring it into manifestation is drawn to it out of the Universal Oneness. The Universal Mind works on it and it comes into being.

This is the key to all prayer work. Praying to make something happen is praying amiss, for such a prayer is not released to God. The person who prays in this manner is simply asking permission to exert his will power in this world with the approval of God. Many people pray this way: "Just give me the approval so that I can use my will power in the way that I see fit. I may step on other people's toes in the process, but I want to be a good boy so give me your approval, God." Yes, we ask and receive not because we ask amiss. We miss the pearl of great price: *That there is that within us which, knowing all things, knows how to bring into expression anything that we need.* It is not only creative, It is dynamic, spontaneous in Its action. It is All-Wise and All-Powerful.

The Joy of Nonresistance

Come unto me, all ye that labour and are heavy laden, and I will give you rest. My yoke is easy and my burden light, said the Master. Why was his burden easy? Because he knew that of himself he did nothing. The Father within did the works.

So often we mortals try to resist the thing out there that is giving us the trouble. What happens? We become more and more involved in the problem. The more we resist it, the bigger it seems. Is there a better way? Yes, the better way is to grow out of it. As we grow in spiritual strength and understanding, giving our attention to the Spirit of Truth within us, the problem fades away.

A good example of this is the person who is unhappy in his job situation. The tendency is to resist the job, the employer, the fellow worker and everything connected with that job. This is not the way to draw a better position into one's experience. First, we must make peace with our environment, trusting and knowing that there is the right and perfect job for us. As long as we resist the outer picture we tend to separate ourselves from the Spirit within. Only through love do we become one with Love. As we turn to the Spirit within, recognizing that it provides us with the capacity to attract a better job, we literally pray our way out of the old situation into the new situation.

Our affairs are our larger body, the "house" that we build through consciousness. Inner resistance breeds outer resistance. If we allow it to continue it magnifies and becomes exaggerated out of all proportion. First, we must find the spiritual growth within. Sometimes it helps to ask: "Father, what is the lesson for me in this situation?" Once the lesson is mastered we need never face it again; but if we manhandle the situation, trying to force our way out of it, we will continue to meet that certain problem again and again. Even to the same personalities. In the past, our tendency has been to try to cure the condition in the outer, which is working on symptoms instead of causes. When Jesus said, *The Father within doeth the works*, he meant that the Perfect Power is within us. The Father knoweth the things we have need of and lovingly provides them, providing the fulfillment of our innermost desires. The Inner Perfection knows how to do all things with ease and with certainty. When we trust It, we work with It and our work ceases to be arduous.

Is There Not Virtue In Work?

Our Puritan ancestors taught us that we must work by the sweat of the brow. They thought it a sin to be idle. There is a subtle difference here and it behooves us to understand it. Work can be a joy. Work can be its own reward — that is, if it is creative work. We can work ten or twelve hours a day if our work is the expression of the divine creativeness in us, and find there is no labor in it. At the end of the day we find ourselves invigorated, filled with zest and enthusiasm. It is not what we do, but how we feel about it. There is no disgrace in physical labor. I know people who have given up office jobs to work with their hands in the fields and loved every minute of it. Only working with distaste, resisting the work, causes people to get tired. As Kahlil Gibran write in the Prophet: *Work is love made visible.*

I remember reading about a man who retired at fifty to do the thing he had always wanted to do. He had spent thirty years in the business world, hating every minute of it, solely for the purpose of making a fortune so that he could afford to do the thing he really wanted to do. This was to have a horse ranch and raise horses. At last, he reached the point where he felt he could afford to stop doing the things he didn't enjoy and start doing the things he'd always wanted to do. To his great surprise he found that he succeeded in his avocation, even more than he had in business. His horse ranch prospered beyond his fondest dreams. To think, he could have done this at any time! He need not have spent all those years doing the thing he didn't enjoy. He only thought it had to be that way. When we are in harmony with the inner Self, work is no longer work; when we express ourselves creatively, work becomes a joy.

We Need Both Mary and Martha

Mary and Martha were sisters. They were the sisters of Lazarus. Jesus often visited in their home.

When he came to see them Mary would sit at his feet while Martha did all of the serving and preparing of the food.

Finally, Martha decided that this thing had gone far enough. She decided to complain to Jesus. She went to him and said: *Lord, dost thou not care that my sister hath left me to serve alone? Bid her, therefore, that she help me.*

She must have been speechless when the Master said to her: *Martha, Martha, thou art careful and troubled about many things, but one thing is needful and Mary hath chosen that good part which shall not be taken away from her.*

What does this mean? It means that Mary had elected to try to understand the spiritual life while Martha was so busy working on the outside, that she did not get a chance. She did not take the opportunity to sit at the feet of the Christ. We often get so involved in the details of living that we lose touch with the greater. I hear the words so often, "I just don't have time to meditate, or to be still." I find that it is fruitless to point out that a day contains 1,440 minutes. If one meditated for 15 minutes, there would still be 1,425 minutes left.

Try making an experiment. For one week, at least, try putting God first. Take a few moments each morning to be still, invoking the Presence of God within you. *Incline thine ear*, as the Bible puts it, and listen for your guidance and your inspiration for the day. You will find that on the days you take time for God, everything falls into place with little effort on your part. You will find that you cannot invest your time better. It is indeed, as Jesus told Martha, *that good part of the day.*

I Will To Will the Will of God

The late Glenn Clark used to say: *"I will to will the will of God."* How does the will of God compare with human will power? The will of God is always in harmony with the nature of God, with all of the attributes of God. It is All-Knowing, All-Wise.

The will of man is apt to be based on resistance and struggle, reflecting his own limited strength and his determination to get his own way. When we depend upon the human will we run into resistance, probably because we expect resistance. We struggle to protect the ego and have our own way.

When we turn to the will of God, there is no resistance, for all of life works with us. The only function of human will power is to keep the attention focused on the Perfect Power within. Each one has within himself a Creative Power beyond anything he can possibly conceive. When we *will to will the will of God* we continually expand our concepts, for we align ourselves with the Infinite.

Now we find that every time we have a new idea, this new idea can be brought into manifestation without struggle or striving. How? By lovingly dwelling upon it and doing all of the things that present themselves as the idea unfolds.

Consider the inventions of man, the various ideas that have been developed through man. How did they come about? By taking the idea and letting it rest in mind, patiently following the instructions that came, one thing leading to another, until eventually the "fruit" was ready to pick. The writer, the inventor, the artist, the scientist, will all tell you that it takes great patience. Those who fail to succeed are not willing to be patient. They want to pick the "fruit" before they plant the seed. It is impossible to hurry the "fruit." If picked too soon it is hard and tasteless. As the farmer awaits the harvest, so must we allow the creative process to take place. Once we are willing to let it work through us we find we can do less and accomplish more. As we so often remind each other: *"There is an easy way and a hard way. God's way is the easy way!"*

Self-Direction for True Prosperity

Today I enter into the consciousness of true prosperity. I disclaim the idea that I am broke, despondent, poor, defeated or disqualified. New opportunities are opening to me.

Whatever I do, I shall do with wisdom, authority, power and right action.

I expect success in all of my undertakings. I know that everything I do will prosper.

I am demonstrating prosperity because there is nothing in me to deny it.

I let blessings, money, and every good thing flow in to me from every direction. I see abundance wherever I look.

A feeling of great serenity and well-being floods my mind. I am guided to do the right thing at the right time.

I am one with my prosperity.

And so it is.

Chapter XI

WRAPPING IT ALL UP

Q. What is prosperity?

A. Prosperity is a state of mind that reflects into every area of living. To prosper means *to be successful, to thrive*. The prosperous person has a feeling that life is working with him and not against him. A prosperity state of mind can produce not only an abundance of wealth but health and right action as well. Money is one of the by-products of prosperity but it is not the only evidence of prosperity thinking.

Q. Is lack or scarcity also a state of mind?

A. Yes. Poverty is not God-ordained. It is the visible manifestation of negative, destructive thinking.

Q. Is there a master key to prosperity?

A. The master key to prosperity is to build a consciousness of prosperity. We must learn to be diligent thought-watchers allowing into our minds only those thoughts that lead to prosperous living. It is a continual mind-training program in which we replace negative, destructive thought patterns with affirmative, constructive thinking.

Q. Where does one start to build a prosperity consciousness?

A. Start right where you are with what you have. Right where you are is a mine of resources more valuable than gold—creative imagination; intuition; creativity; love; understanding; ideas; inspiration and more. Start with what you have and move confidently forward.

Q. Are there practical steps that will help one build a prosperity consciousness?

A. Yes, here are practical steps that you can take:

1. Make an inventory of all of your assets; spiritual, mental and physical.

2. Check out your options without judgment. Make a list of them. You may have more opportunities than you think.

3. If you are job-hunting, start visualizing yourself as doing the thing you most want to do. Then, take all of the human footsteps necessary to find that job.

4. Set goals and mentally walk through them as if you had already attained them.

5. Mentally accept the best and you will have the best; expect the best and you will get the best.

Q. Is the possession of money and things the criterion of prosperity?

A. Absolutely not. Many people who are considered to be rich really have a consciousness of poverty. Fear of losing what one has is poverty itself.

Q. Who are the rich? Who are the poor?

A. A person who is afraid to use his money, hiding it under the mattress, denying himself the comforts of life, is really poor; while a person who lives within his means even if on a limited retirement income may, for all practical purposes, feel rich.

Q. What are some of the pitfalls to prosperity?

A. There are a number of pitfalls that will keep one from demonstrating prosperity.

1. Trying to get something for nothing.
2. Feeling unworthy to receive one's good.
3. Being a pocketbook protector.
4. Making an enemy out of one's competitor.
5. Getting yours while the getting's good.
6. Leaners who dare not trust the Perfect Power within.
7. Hating to pay the bills and the taxes.
8. Fear of losing what we have.
9. Thinking that there is a virtue in poverty.
10. Accepting poverty as one's destiny.

Q. Is it possible to change the direction of one's thinking enough to bring about success and prosperity in life?

A. Yes, this is a law of life. Whenever a person is willing to change his thinking, giving new conscious direction to his subconscious mind, there is bound to be a change in the outer experience.

Q. How does one go about giving new direction to the subconscious mind?

A. Self-Direction is the art of directing the subconscious mind into channels of right use. *That which a person believes about himself and confidently expects, will become his experience.*

Affirmations are constructive statements phrased in the first person. They help one establish a new order of thinking. Keep reviewing the Self-Direction affirmations at the end of each chapter.

A seven-day mental diet (see Chapter V) is a great help in retraining the subsonscious mind.

Meditation is a wonderful means of mind-cleansing. Meditation puts us in tune with Life and when we are in tune all of Life works with us.

Flash cards can be of great help — little wallet-size cards with statements of truth affirmations on them.

Mental treatments for prosperity such as those in our book, YOUR NEEDS MET, will help you overcome negative thought patterns and build a consciousness of prosperity.

Q. What do we mean by creative imagination?

A. Creative imagination is using the imagination creatively to envision that which we desire to experience.

Q. Is it possible to use creative imagination erroneously?

A. Yes, by picturing in our minds situations that we really do not want to experience.

Q. How does one use creative imagination?

A. Creative imagination is a form of prayer. Jesus was referring to creative imagination when he said:

> *What things soever ye desire, when ye pray, believe that ye receive them and ye shall have them.*

The farmer uses creative imagination when he plants the corn. He envisions the time of harvest.

The salesman uses creative imagination when he pictures himself successfully closing the sale.

Q. What do we mean by *doing first things first*?

A. Make a list of the things that need to be done in the order of their importance. Keep doing the most important thing first, crossing off each item as accomplished. You will find this takes the feeling of frustration out of the situation and enables you *to do first things first*.

Q. What are some of the laws of life that can work for us?

A. We live in a universe of law and order. There are definite laws that apply to every activity in life. They will work for us or against us depending upon how we use them. These laws are impersonal. They do not care how we use them. It is up to us. Some of them are:

1. The law of identification—whatever we identify ourselves with we become.
2. The law of attraction—we draw into our experience that which we believe and accept for ourselves.
3. The law of cause and effect—for every cause there is an effect and for every effect there is a cause. A thought can be a cause in mind which produces an effect in the outer experience.
4. The law of increase—that to which we give our attention is bound to increase.
5. The law of giving and receiving. Only when we give are we able to receive.

Q. Why is the law of giving and receiving important where prosperity is concerned?

A. Because all of life is in continual circulation. If we do not give back into life we interfere with and eventually dam up the circulatory activity. Giving is the basis for building a prosperity consciousness.

Q. Why is it important to be a good receiver?

A. Because a good receiver is keeping the circulatory activity of life open. Prosperous people are good receivers. They have learned to receive their good and be grateful for it. Learning to receive starts with gratitude and giving thanks is a continual recognition of the infinite Source of our good.

Q. Is it possible to build a consciousness of uninterrupted prosperity?

A. Yes, it is possible and here are two steps to take:
  1. Learn to live within your means. Feast-or-famine spending develops a feast-or-famine pattern that soon causes one to feel poor. Putting something aside for the future tends to give one a feeling of plenty.
  2. Start a tithing program on a regular basis. This is a continual reminder that the infinite Source never runs out. It's fun to give God's money and it makes you feel rich. When you feel rich you draw riches to you.

Q. Why does tithing bring about such a great change in the mental attitude of the tither?

A. Tithing is an act of faith, a proving up of one's faith. Tithing is the evidence of spiritual growth as it pertains to supply. Tithing causes one to change one's feeling about money.

Q. What are some of the effects the individual may look for after starting a tithing program?

A. To give trustingly to God's work, without thought of gain; to give with no strings attached, simply for the joy of giving, builds a consciousness of trusting in the infinite Source. Because the Source is infinite the reaping can be infinite.

   1. When the tither expands his awareness, there is an increase in his outer experience.

   2. Even the regular income seems to go farther.

   3. The tithe may start to return to the tither multiplied.

   4. Funds are available from completely unexpected avenues.

Q. To whom should the tithe be given?

A. Where do you receive your spiritual inspiration? Give the tithe to God's work according to your own inner guidance.

Q. Must one start with the full ten percent tithe?

A. Not everyone is ready for the full tithe. This comes with spiritual growth and is usually a gradual unfoldment. Some start out with a partial tithe. This may be a quarter tithe or a half tithe. When the tither finds that he or she cannot outgive God it becomes easy to give the full ten percent.

Q. Why is it that tithing seems to work such magic in our lives?

A. Because tithing is a spiritual discipline that constantly reminds us that God is our supply. As we continually turn to the Source trusting and knowing that our good is not withheld we gradually overcome our fear of lack.

Q. Why do some people feel guilty about being prosperous?

A. Many people have picked up the idea that there is some virtue in being poor. The reason for this may be that these people think that the only way to get wealth is to take it away from somebody else. When we are able to accept our supply as a gift from God we develop an entirely different feeling about wealth.

Q. Is it possible to be prosperous and still put God first?

A. The answer is an emphatic "yes," for this is the only way to develop true prosperity. The Bible is full of references to prosperity which is promised to those who keep the first commandment — put God first.

Q. What is spiritual prosperity and what are some of the effects in our lives?

A. When we put God first and become one with His Life the flow of good from unexpected channels sometimes comes so fast it astounds us. The key word here is *let*. *Let* it happen. *Let* your supply flow unimpeded to the glory of God.

Spiritual prosperity is a state of mind that projects itself into one's circumstances so that every part of life reflects this state of mind.

The truly prosperous are at peace with themselves and others, at ease in all situations, free of resentment, hate or greed.

Wealth and health and a general state of well-being are by-products of true prosperity.

Spiritual prosperity must begin with faith in the Source of all good to supply our needs. Our security must be an inner condition that is not affected by outer conditions. True wealth is of the Spirit.

Q. How does one invest in true prosperity?

A. Investing in true prosperity is an inner experience. It is a gradual process that develops with spiritual enlightenment. It starts the moment a person turns to the Source, trusting and knowing that God is his supply. When one invests in spiritual prosperity everything else falls into place easily: the right position, right guidance and right action. Just the right people are drawn to us. All that is needed for the manifestation of prosperity comes easily and happily.

Q. What is *the law of effortless action*?

A. By this we mean how to accomplish more with less effort. When we put God first and let the divine law guide and direct our steps we cease to exert our human efforts in what seems to be the obvious way and instead we ask for guidance and let the creative process direct our steps. It becomes what we might call *effortless action*.

Q. What is the creative process and how does it work?

A. The subconscious mind responds to conscious direction. Therefore, that which you contemplate becomes the law of your being and is brought forth into manifestion. You do not have to do anything about it except let go and let God create through you. You do not make the wheat grow, you only plant the seed. You do not build your body but you plant the thought seed.

Chapter XII

PRACTICAL APPLICATION

Fifteen Keys To Prosperity

Here are 15 Keys to prosperous living. These keys will open doors for you. Be courageous in walking through those doors. Otherwise, you will be on the outside looking in.

"The great end of life is not knowledge but action," said Thomas Huxley. Use these 15 Keys to build your confidence and faith, *then dare to act upon it.*

1. Prosperity Is a State of Mind

Remember, prosperity really is a state of mind. And so is poverty. Resolve to build a consciousness of abundance and prosperity through constructive and positive thinking.

Affirm Daily:

I am prosperity. All that the Father has is mine. My good flows to me from an infinite Source. Everything I do or say increases my prosperity.

2. Start Where You Are With What You Have

What do you have? Right where you are is a mine of resources more valuable than gold.

You have creative imagination. You have intuition to guide you and creativity to build whatever it is you may need or want. Right within you is a reservoir of love and understanding that can overcome any problem and inspiration that will move hearts as well as mountains. Start with what you have and move forward.

Affirm Daily:
The Presence of God at the center of my being fills my every need. My cup runneth over.

3. Do It Now
You can do it. Whatever it is that you need to do, you can do it. And the way *to do* it, is *to do* it. Not just look at it or talk about it. Think the thing through and then move on it. You may not realize it but you have what it takes. You are greater than you think. Emerson said, "Do the thing and you will have the power." He was a wise man.

Affirm Daily:
Through the Perfect Power within me I am able to move mountains. Nothing is too hard for God.

4. That To Which You Give Your Attention Grows and Multiplies
That which the Spirit contemplates, it becomes—*and God said, Let there be light*. God in you is Spirit individualized. God creates

through you that to which you give your attention. That which you contemplate becomes the law of your being. That which you contemplate is brought forth into manifestation. The choice is yours. You can think about poverty or you can think about prosperity.

Affirm Daily:

I am ruling out all thoughts of lack. I choose to give my attention to abundance and prosperity; enough and to spare, to give and to share.

5. Move Confidently Toward Your Heart's Desire

One of the most common stumbling blocks to prosperity is lack of self-motivation. Getting started on a prosperity program becomes easy when you learn to be your own self-directed motivator.

By writing out your directions in advance you will have to think things through and this leads to good results. This is a great way to motivate yourself. *Do not depend upon others to motivate you.* Do not turn this leadership over to another.

Affirm Daily:

All of the Power and Intelligence of God is expressing through me. I move confidently toward my heart's desire. I trust the creativity of Life. All that I need is right where I am.

6. Our Prosperity Does Not Depend Upon Others

Life is an individual experience. You and only you can live your life. Whatever you find to do, do it with all your might. Beware of depending on the benevolence of others, or some special privilege or upon some relative or upon a union. It's more interesting and rewarding to do your job as though you were in business for yourself. Enthusiasm, willingness and hard work are the foundation stones of a job well done.

Affirm Daily:

God is my supply, an infinite Source right within me. All that I need flows through me. I dare to depend upon the infinite Source of all good to provide for my every need. I accept my good from all of life. I do not depend on others, I depend on God.

7. Give and You Shall Receive

Jesus stated a Law of Life when he said; *Give and it shall be given unto you; good measure, pressed down, and shaken together, and running over, shall men give into your bosom. For with the same measure that ye mete withal it shall be measured to you again.*

What shall you give? What do you have? Give freely of your time, your wisdom, your skills, your labor, and, of course, your money.

Feel free to help others. Whatever you give, give it freely and joyously. Don't keep mental books to see if what you give comes back to you. Trust Life to give you a bountiful return.

Remember: YOU CAN'T OUTGIVE GOD!

Affirm Daily:

I give unstintingly into life, drawing always from the infinite Source. I give joyously with an awareness of abundance.

8. Expect the Best and You Will Get the Best

We have to expect the best in order to receive the best. Start by knowing that consciousness is the only reality. If you have a consciousness of success, that which you accept for yourself will become your experience. If you desire to prosper, know that prosperity is a matter of having a prosperity consciousness. Once you have established a prosperity consciousness, nothing can take it away from you. You will never lack any good thing.

Affirm Daily:

Divine good is living all around me and expressing through me. I am a center of divine good. I expect the best and I receive the best. Only good goes from me and only good returns to me.

9. Use the Best and You Will Always Have the Best

A young man was eating from a plate of grapes when the rabbi came to call. He asked the rabbi, "Shouldn't I always save the best grapes for the last?"

The rabbi surprised him by saying, "Always eat the best first, and you'll always be eating the best."

Use the best you have and you will always have the best because you will be building a prosperity consciousness as you go.

Affirm Daily:

My Father is a millionaire. He wants me to have the best. I accept the best and use the best without guilt or regret.

10. Prosperity Does Not Depend Upon Overcoming Competition

There is one pitfall to our prosperity that we are apt to overlook because it is disguised as a great American virtue. It is known as competition. "All's fair in love and war," they say. Many think the same applies in business; that business is a sort of war against the competition.

Actually, it is a proven fact that we only compete against ourselves. The new supermarket across the street will draw new customers into the area and help each little store in the neighborhood.

Affirm Daily:

I bless my competition for I know that there is no competition in the One Mind. Their success is my success. Their good is my good. Their prosperity is also possible for me. I rejoice in my competitor's good as I welcome it into my own experience.

11. Fear of Poverty is Poverty Itself

There are two approaches to life: the prosperity approach and the poverty approach. Some people take the attitude that because of their background, their environment, their nationality, or some other self-manufactured reason, they are destined to be poverty-ridden all of their lives. Others live in poverty when they don't have to.

Affirm Daily:

Life's free-flowing abundance is mine to use and to share. I need no longer store it up in fear for I trust the fresh manna for tomorrow.

12. Be Glad to Pay Your Bills and Other Obligations

Here's a pitfall with which we're all familiar: hating to pay the bills, hating to pay those taxes, putting off writing the checks as long as possible because we hate to see our bank account diminished. This is a subtle snare and one we should be aware of. It stems from a mistaken belief that our Source will become depleted.

We have a little game that we play at our house. When we write our checks, instead of writing 00/100's after the dollars, we write OO/xxx, and we know as we write those three little xxx's that they mean "God is Abundance."

Affirm Daily:

I gladly pay each bill with a special blessing for the receiver. I gladly pay my taxes. Instead of thinking of government expenditures with which I disagree, I give my attention to the good public works with which I can agree. I bless each check knowing that that which I give freely will come back to me in the same way. I am spending out of my consciousness of abundance.

13. Let Your Creativity Open Up New Avenues of Income

Each person is unique in body, mind and spirit. No two people express life in exactly the same way. Each person is endowed with an infinite Source of creativity, imagination, unlimited ideas that can be turned into prosperity.

God works for us, through us. The ideas are given to us but they must be carried out through us. God's abundance is your abundance. It flows through mind into manifestation. God gives you the necessary ideas and clothes them with all that is needed to bring them into form when we ask believing.

Affirm Daily:

I choose to look at my assets instead of my liabilities. Nothing can interfere with the perfect right action of God within me. I refuse to be governed by the past. Circumstances have no power over me. I let my creativity open up new avenues of income for me. Ideas come to me at the right and perfect time. I act upon these ideas with confidence and assurance.

14. Feel Worthy of Being Prosperous

It is surprising to me how many people feel unworthy of prosperity.

The young man who inherited a fortune and threw it away in the streets that he might himself join the less fortunate accomplished no lasting good. He simply established the fact that he did not have a consciousness of prosperity. Good stewardship requires that we accept the responsibility to use what is entrusted to us in a wise and intelligent way.

Affirm Daily:

God plays no favorites. I am worthy of receiving prosperity. I accept my good as it freely
flows to me. I give freely and receive freely,
knowing God is the Source of my supply.

15. Seek Ye First the Kingdom of God and All of These Things Shall Be Added

*Seek ye first the kingdom of God and its
righteousness* (the right use of the Law) *and all
of these things shall be added unto you.* What
things? Why, the simple things, food, shelter,
and clothing. All that you need. The Master
said that all of these things would be taken care
of by the heavenly Father who knows that we
have need of these things. He said that we need
not struggle and strive any more than the lilies
of the field.

Life will provide for us as we are willing to
accept our good in consciousness. It is not a
matter of getting but of giving into life knowing that life will give back to us. Yes, all of the
things will be added unto us.

Affirm Daily:

I seek inner dominion through the Spirit
within, knowing that my prosperity is founded
on dominion through inner power.

Daily Affirmations For A
Month Of Prosperous Living

1. Prosperity exists. Prosperity exists for me. I accept prosperity as my way of life.

2. Everywhere I look, I see evidence of abundance. I am one with abundance. Prosperity is the law of my life.

3. I do not depend on "luck." I depend on the One Source for my unfailing prosperity.

4. I rejoice in the prosperity of others. I rejoice in accepting prosperity for myself. I am prosperity.

5. That which I think about becomes my experience. I choose to think thoughts of prosperity, abundance and opulence.

6. Money is not evil, only the inordinate love of money is evil. All that I need comes to me at the right time, in the right way.

7. There is no virtue in being stingy. The Lord loves a cheerful giver. I give freely and generously.

8. Hoarding is not prospering. I am an open channel for good. Only good goes from me and only good returns to me.

9. There is no virtue in being poor. There is virtue in being a good steward. I am a good steward of God's abundance.

10. Prosperity is only an instrument to be used, not a deity to be worshipped. I worship God within, the Source of all good.

11. I seek first the kingdom of divine good within and its right use, knowing that all that I need is added unto me.

12. I give freely and receive joyfully out of a sense of abundance. I receive my good gladly, allowing others the joy of giving.

13. My abundance is from God. There is no power in lack. I use God's gifts wisely and joyfully.

14. When I think of the wonder of God's life around and through me, how can I lack? I live in the midst of plenty and I prosper in all that I do.

15. As I tithe I prosper. In the spirit that I give to God, God gives to me. I give freely and joyfully out of a grateful heart.

16. My word for good renders prosperous everything I undertake. My feeling of inner wealth neutralizes any suggestion of lack.

17. I am employed by God who rewards my services with lavish praise and generous remuneration. I think prosperity, I speak prosperity. I am prosperity.

18. I believe in God's abundance. Prosperity is the spiritual approach to God's bounty.

19. I start where I am with what I have and give thanks to God. I move forward creatively to accomplish the tasks of this day.

20. I prosper in my relationship with others. I like people and look forward to making new friends. I prosper in all that I undertake.

21. Every dollar I circulate enriches the economy and comes back to me multiplied, for God gives the increase.

22. Prosperity means more than wealth — it means health, happiness and success made manifest. It means life is working with me and I am working with life.

23. Prosperity means, according to your desire with expectation: to turn out well; to increase; to thrive; to grow; to be fortunate.

24. There is a law of life that whatever we expect will become our experience. I expect prosperity and prosperity is my experience.

25. I rejoice and give thanks for the bountiful life within and around me. There is no limit to God's Abundance.

26. The law of attraction works for me by filling my every need as it becomes known to me. I attract good because I open my mind to receive good.

27. I am secure in the knowledge that God, infinite life, is the continual source of my supply. "I shall not want."

28. I give thanks for inner resources: imagination, intuition, and creativity. These are gifts from God and they add to my prosperity. I am prosperity.

29. Adversities met are the sinews of prosperity. I have now learned all that I need to know through adversity. I prosper in peace.

30. Prosperity is a state of mind. It is a state of being prosperous, to advance or gain in anything good. I am prosperity.

31. As I prosper I give thanks to God, the Source of all good. I rejoice in helping others prosper through the power of God.

A Treatment For
Unexpected Money

God has ways to bless me I know not of.
  I EXPECT THE UNEXPECTED!

Life flows through me into bountiful expression.
  I EXPECT THE UNEXPECTED!

Windows of heaven are open, blessings pour out.
  I EXPECT THE UNEXPECTED!

Everywhere I look, life's plenty astounds me.
  I EXPECT THE UNEXPECTED!

I am one with Life and Life is one with me.
  I EXPECT THE UNEXPECTED!

God wants me to be happy and fulfilled.
  I EXPECT THE UNEXPECTED!

Whatever blesses one person blesses us all.
  I EXPECT THE UNEXPECTED!

Whatever happens to another can happen to me.
  I EXPECT THE UNEXPECTED!

Nothing is denied me. Life works with me.
  I EXPECT THE UNEXPECTED!

My prosperity comes to me many ways.
UNEXPECTED MONEY IS ONE OF THEM.

I accept my good, the good that is known and the
good that is yet to be revealed.
I give thanks that it is so.

Some Common Fallacies
Concerning Prosperity

1. It is a fallacy to think that prosperity depends on luck.

2. It is a fallacy to think that prosperity depends upon the ability to get money.

3. It is a fallacy to think that money is evil.

4. It is a fallacy to think that it is wicked to be rich.

5. It is a fallacy to think that it is a virtue to be stingy.

6. It is a fallacy to think that the economic system is faulty and that therefore it is impossible to be prosperous.

7. It is a fallacy to think that the government will take it all away in taxes, therefore one cannot prosper.

8. It is a fallacy to think that prosperous living depends upon storing up goods or money for the future.

9. It is a fallacy to think that there is a virtue in poverty.

10. It is a fallacy to think that one is unworthy to receive.

11. It is a fallacy to be a martyr, trying to prove that life is against one.

12. It is a fallacy to think that one has to be grim to be prosperous.

Diet For Prosperity

Everywhere we turn today, people are diet-conscious. Each new diet that comes along promises to work wonders. There is an old saying: "You are what you eat." This, of course, pertains to the food that goes into our mouths.

But, still more important, "You are what you think." Your mental diet determines your life experience. Any thought that is not positive and constructive, whether it concerns you or someone else, is a negative thought. Any thought of limitation or lack will reflect as limitation in your affairs. It is therefore very important to choose a good mental diet for prosperity that is designed to restructure your thinking.

Just as with a food diet it is important to rule out certain foods, we are going to rule out certain negative thoughts relating to prosperity.

Just imagine yourself sitting in front of a big, warm, cozy fire on a winter's night. A coal pops out of the fire and lands on the sleeve of your best coat. Immediately you knock it off before it has a chance to burn a hole in your coat. During these seven days of your mental diet for prosperity, think of any thought of lack or limitation as a hot coal. If such a thought pops up in your mind, immediately reverse it and declare its opposite, a positive, affirmative idea. This is going to take discipline, but you will find it well worth it. The rewards will be great.

Instructions:

Here are seven key ideas, one for each day of the week. You may start on any day. Call that your first day. Memorize your key idea and live with it that day. Say it over and over as many times as you can, every hour, on the hour, if you can. Be faithful for seven days and you will make these strong ideas your own. Expect your circumstances to change for that which you partake of mentally *will become your experience*.

7-Day Mental Diet for Prosperity

First Day:

    Divine Love expressing through me now draws to me all that I need to make my life complete and fulfilled.

Second Day:

    I desire the highest and best in life and I draw the highest and best to me.

Third Day:

    My good comes to me with perfect timing according to God's perfect plan for me.

Fourth Day:

Divine Intelligence is in charge of my life. I am open, receptive and obedient to its rich instruction and guidance.

Fifth Day:

I am now activated by Divine Intelligence, motivated by Divine Love, and guided by Divine Power into paths of success and perfect right action.

Sixth Day:

All that I need is mine to use, share, and exchange according to the law of divine circulation.

Seventh Day:

Money is God's Love in expression. Since it is never withheld from me I dare to give freely of all that comes to me from the one Infinite Source.

8 Steps To Opulent Living

1. Think, I AM PROSPEROUS, over and over until you are able to accept the idea for yourself.

2. Think over and over, MY EVERY THOUGHT LEADS ME TO OPULENT LIVING.

3. Think over and over, MY EVERY ACT LEADS ME TO OPULENT LIVING. Work on these ideas until you have established them in your subconscious mind.

4. Affirm the following statements again and again until they have routed out of your thinking all poverty thoughts: I RENOUNCE AND DISCOURAGE ALL THOUGHTS OF LACK, ENTERTAINING HENCEFORTH ONLY THOUGHTS OF ABUNDANT GOOD.

5. I AM CREATIVE WHEN I NEED TO BE CREATIVE.

6. I AM PRODUCTIVE WHEN I NEED TO BE PRODUCTIVE.

7. I GIVE OF MYSELF UNSTINTINGLY INTO LIFE, DRAWING ALWAYS FROM AN INFINITE SOURCE.

8. I BUILD A CONSCIOUSNESS OF ABUN-DANCE BY GIVING BACK TO THE SOURCE 1/10th OF MY INCOME. I GIVE FROM AN INFINITE SOURCE, THE SOURCE OF ALL GOOD. (Give your tithe to whatever spiritual work from which you receive inspiration. If you give with a true motive you will find that this is the secret of true wealth.)

ABOUT THE AUTHORS

For more than 30 years the Addingtons have worked closely together in the fields of writing and lecturing. Through its monthly publication, the Abundant Living magazine, Abundant Living Foundation brings their teaching to thousands of people throughout the world.

Jack Addington attended the University of Florida at Gainesville, and has had three successful careers, first in business where he was a practicing attorney, then 20 years in the ministry, founding two large churches. In 1969 he retired from church work to begin his worldwide ministry. He now devotes his time to writing, lecturing, a large radio and prayer ministry, and his work in the prisons.

Cornelia Addington attended the University of Washington in Seattle where she majored in painting and design. She was successful as a designer for a large manufacturing firm, later going into interior design. During the past 30 years she has edited Dr. Addington's manuscripts and co-authored several of his books. She is the editor of the Abundant Living magazine and has had numerous articles published in national magazines.